# Bye-Bye AMERICA:

## I Found a Better Home

*To Eric From Earle "All life's best!"*

# EARLE F. ZEIGLER

## 2013

### PUBLISHED BY FIDELI PUBLISHING INC.

ISBN: 978-1-60414-743-8

Cover Photographyt & Design by: Andy Naval
**www.accugraphics.ca**

# Dedication

This book is dedicated to those millions of Americans who feel exactly as I do about the developing situation in America. Unfortunately they are trapped with no way out... Moreover untold millions don't even understand what has happened. I was lucky, I guess... I only hope that *somehow* those left there through their dedicated efforts will be able to improve the situation somewhat for the sake of their families and offspring..

# Contents

*Dedication*................................................................................................*iii*

*Preface*...................................................................................................*vii*

*Prologue*................................................................................................*xiii*

Speculation About the Future............................................................... xvi

## PART I

**The World and America** ....................................................................... 1

Introduction ....................................................................................... 1

Significant Developments Have "Transformed Our Lives".................... 2

The World Has Three Major Trading Blocks........................................ 3

The Impact of Negative Social Forces Has Increased. ......................... 6

Megalopolis Living Problems Are Far From Being Solved ................... 6

Technology and Life Improvement...................................................... 7

What Character Do We Seek for People? ............................................ 8

Postmodernism as an Influence.......................................................... 9

What Happened to the Original Enlightenment Ideal?...................... 12

## PART II

**Life Before the Illinois Scandal** ......................................................... 14

My "Beginning" in New York City ................................................... 14

The "Great Depression Years"........................................................... 18

High School in Norwalk, CT ........................................................... 20

Bates College "Rah, Rah"! (1936-40) .............................................. 21

Graduate School (Herr Zeigler!) ...................................................... 27

My First Position: Y.M.C.A. Secretary............................................. 29

Position #2: Yale University ............................................................. 30

Eyeball Flaw a Determining Factor .................................................. 35

That's Me "All Over"… .................................................................... 37

Getting That "Union Card": the Ph.D. ............................................ 38

My First Publication ........................................................................ 46

How I Happened to Move to Canada ........................................ 47

The Idea of a "Unified Program" ............................................ 51

Back to America: "Go Blue" ................................................. 52

Staley and Illinois Physical Education Development ..................... 55

From Ann Arbor, MI to Urbana. IL ........................................ 56

**PART III**

**"The Illinois Slush-Fund Scandal"** ...................................... **59**

Announcement of the "Irregularities ...................................... 59

The Big Ten Investigation: Search for a New Athletic Director ........ 61

The Search for New Coaches ............................................... 65

Results of NCAA Deliberations ............................................ 66

Discussion ................................................................. 67

Concluding Statement ...................................................... 69

Reference Notes ........................................................... 69

References ................................................................ 70

**PART IV**

**Life After the Illinois "Debacle"** ...................................... **72**

"Canada, Here We Come Back Again"! ...................................... 74

A Mere Full Professor Once Again… ........................................ 79

A Year As a "Traveling Scholar" .......................................... 82

Resumption of "Life As Usual" ............................................ 86

"Where Do We Go From Here?" .............................................. 92

Special Recognitions for Professional Service ........................... 93

Fate Steps In ............................................................. 95

I Meet Anne Rogers! ...................................................... 96

Remarks at 90th Birthday Party on August 20, 2009 ...................... 98

The "Last Best Hope" on Earth? .......................................... 100

PART V

**Counteracting America's Value Orientation** ............................ **107**
    Introduction ................................................................... 107
    Future Societal Scenarios (Anderson) .................................... 111
    What Kind of A World Do You Want for Your Descendants? ............... 113
    How We Might Improve the Planet ....................................... 116
    Can We Strengthen the Postmodern Influence? .......................... 120

**Epilogue** ........................................................................ **128**

**Developmental Physical Activity Should Create Positive Values... 129**
    This Disoriented Field Involving Human Physical Activity Should Have a
        Mission? ................................................................... 130

**Based on Established Principles, We Should Guarantee the Best
Type of Developmental Physical Activity to Youth** ..................... **135**
    Physical Activity Education's Fourteen (14) "Principal Principles" ........... 135
    The Professional Task Ahead ............................................. 137
    What Should The Field of Developmental Physical Activity Do
        in the 21st Century? ...................................................... 138

**Babe Ruth or Lou Gehrig: An American Dilemma** ..................... **146**

**America Is Screwing Up Physical (Activity) Education and
(Educational) Sport** ............................................................ **150**

**A Clash of Moral and Socio-Instrumental Values:
Tiger Woods Caught In a Vise** ................................................ **152**
    Challenging the Role of Sport in Society .................................. 153
    "Socio-Instrumental" Values or "Moral" Values? ......................... 156
    Concluding Statement .................................................... 157

**Semi-ProfessIonal Sport Does Not a Great University Make ....... 159**

On What Basis Might a Country Sponsor the Olympic Games?.............. 162

The Problem .................................................................................. 163

An Assessment of the Problem. ....................................................... 164

Concluding Statement ..................................................................... 166

References ..................................................................................... 166

**Sport in the Postmodern World ............................................. 168**

Naipaul or Huntington: "Universal Civilization or the Clash of
    Civilizations?.......................................................................... 169

The "Tragic Sense" of Life (Muller)................................................. 171

The "Plight" of Sport Management.................................................. 172

Characterizations of Competitive Sport........................................... 174

Is Sport Fulfilling Its Presumed Educational and Recreational Roles
    Adequately? ........................................................................... 175

Official Sport's Response to the Prevailing Situation ....................... 178

What Kind of A World Do You Want for Your Descendants?............ 184

Concluding Statement ..................................................................... 186

References ..................................................................................... 187

# Preface

The title of this book should not be confusing. First I state that I *must* "say goodbye" to living and working in America. The second half of the title is straightforward as well. Why did I say "goodbye"? Because something went terribly wrong where I was working. Fortunately I did indeed find a comparable academic position in Canada, and I also did indeed "find a better home" there too!

To explain further, my career had been brought to a standstill in a major university in America—University of Illinois, UIUC—by what was called "The Illinois Slush-Fund Scandal". Three coaches with who held part-time, academic appointments in the department I headed were accused of serious infractions of

the rules of the National Collegiate Athletic Association. Yet I, as their department head, could not find out anything about the situation. Everything (!) went immediately to the President's Office. The only ongoing information I received was by reading two of the local newspapers in Champaign-Urbana, Illinois…

This deplorable situation soon brought me to a state where I almost got an ulcer because of concern over the matter. Hence, after talking it over with my wife, I decided that I must step down from my administrative post—and then move elsewhere as soon as possible. Sadly, I soon realized that there was no closely identical *academic* position available in any top-flight university that wasn't also similarly involved with over-emphasized, professionalized intercollegiate athletics.

(The Ivy League doesn't offer professional preparation in physical activity education including sport).

What could I do? What should I do? Fortunately, I discovered that Canada—where I had worked previously in the early 1950s—had now progressed to the point educationally that the academic position I aspired to at that point in my career was available in a university that had not "sold its educational soul to the almighty dollar"!

Also, as it has turned out, I discovered that Canada is indeed a much better place to live! To explain further: My basic concern—the one that brought about a second—and final!—move to Canada related to what was happening in my field of physical activity education (including so-called educational sport). Additionally, as I sadly and gradually came to accept, the overall situation in America had become so grim that I took out Canadian citizenship as well. Today I just don't see how what has been the world's leading country (America!) can ever recover from the myriad problems that continuing unwise decisions have forced upon it...

Hence, what I have done by writing and publishing this book is to unofficially—but literally in many ways—publish my "goodbye" to the country of my birth. This was not an easy thing to do. I confess to having had extremely mixed feelings as I wrote this book. The large majority of my relatives, friends, and associates—alive or dead—were or are Americans. A number of them knew that what I was doing when I left the first time in 1949 was only to get ahead in my field. Yet then, when I left for a second time in 1971 at age 54 to become dean of a new college ("faculty "as termed in America!) in a Canadian university, undoubtedly many others just shook their heads... In a way I did feel like a traitor! Still I felt that I had no other choice. Most probably thought: "I guess the 'aging fool' knows what he's doing. However, 'up there' in a nondescript Canada is where he'll end up..."

As it happened, the earlier seven-year period spent at The University of Western Ontario between 1949 and 1956 had been a wonderful experience until 1956. Then the president and I had a disagreement about the length and content of the physical education requirement still in force there after World War II.

As it happened, also, I was the only American department head out of 22 such administrators—and a very young one at that. Even though in a sense I was a "babe in the woods", my assignment there had been most interesting to me. In addition to teaching courses a variety of theory and practice course in the professional program for physical activity and health educators, at various times I also coached the line in football and alternately coached the university swimming and wrestling teams.

Yet, most fortunately as it happened, in 1956 Paul Hunsicker, a friend and professional colleague at The University of Michigan, Ann Arbor, "rescued me" from the "declining situation" in my field at Western University (as it is now called officially) in London, Ontario, Canada. Fortunately for me, he was able to do so because he was just about to assume the department headship at the University of Michigan, Ann Arbor. Subsequently everything went along just fine in Ann Arbor as I matured in my profession and also became somewhat of a scholar. This was required to ensure promotion to a higher rank, and I enjoyed it. Soon I was elected also to membership in what is now called the National Academy of Kinesiology, an honorary group of 100 scholars in the field of kinesiology and physical activity education.

However, there was one potential problem at The University of Michigan that I soon began to understand—but only superficially at first. (Doesn't it seem as if there is always one problem "out there" at any or all stages of life and living?) I should explain that in this situation I was actually listed as a professor in the School of Education for the professional preparation aspects of my position, but our unit was also very closely associated with the Intercollegiate Athletics Department of the University. And, as it happened, the required physical education program for all students, including intramural athletics, was assigned to that administrative unit of the institution.

Intercollegiate athletics was, and is still today, an important part of The University of Michigan. How important, and the many potential ramifications of the overall situation in athletics in American higher education, I confess that I did not fully understand at that time when I worked there from 1956 to 1963. Oh,

I remember how Fritz Crisler, the athletic director (and former football coach!), in an adjoining building, was looked upon as some sort of a mysterious God-like figure. And I recall further the upset created when Andy Kozar, a former all-American fullback from Tennessee and the (Ph.D. graduate-student) instructor in one of our professional courses gave grades of "C' to some varsity football players. Hence he was immediately removed from that assignment! And I remember still further the unusual number of athletes who majored in astronomy studying with an elderly female professor who often went along with the team on away trips. Her typical grading pattern was "A" for athletes, "B" for boys, and "C" for coeds.

Nevertheless, it hadn't sunk in on me yet the extent to which "American football" and "varsity sport" "ruled the roost" in Division I and Division II universities that came under the auspices of the National Collegiate Athletic Association. It was somehow destined to take longer for me to truly understand, because I had previously taught and coached football and swimming at Yale University where the situation was fundamentally different. "How so?" you may ask. Yale, in the so-called Ivy League and a world-famous institution, is still today a Division III institution within the National Collegiate Athletic Association.

What does that Division III status mean? Simply this: In Division III colleges and universities, athletes receive financial help (1) if they are bona fide students and (2) if the need for financial aid is *proven*! Conversely, the situation with financial aid in Division I and II institutions may in a number of instances be likened to "professional" and "semi-professional" status respectively—an exaggeration, of course, but not too far off in a number of situations. Also, the scholarly endeavor of many of these "scholarship athletes" often leaves much to be desired—as the many exposes over the years have shown.

Interestingly, it wasn't until I became department head at the University of Illinois in 1963 that I began to understand what was "going on" at the upper level of American intercollegiate athletics. Ten such understanding sunk in decisively when the "Illinois slush fund scandal" broke in 1967. There were 17 coaches on my departmental payroll in the physical education unit anywhere from 10 percent to 75 percent F.T.E. In total, there were 130 people on the payroll, including instructors and graduate assistants. And these figures were just for the men's department; so, obviously, it was a very large program. (Note: there will be a detailed discussion of this sad tale in Part III of the book.)

When this scandal developed, the head and assistant basketball coaches, and the head football coach, were caught up in the imbroglio. Also, I discovered right off that I could not find out anything about it! "Everything!" went immediately and completely into the Office of the President. So I said to Dean McCristal of our College of Physical Education: "We've got to get to the bottom of this. How are we going to break tenure on these people if they're proven guilty?" I can remember good, old King McCristal replying, "I'll make an appointment with President Henry." A bit later, on the way over to our meeting, King said, "Don't disagree with President Henry about anything." I turned around and started walking the other way just "for the hell of it". "Where are you going, where are you going?" he said. I replied: "There's no point in going to have an interview if I can't respond to what I might disagree with." "Well, he said, just be very gentle about it because university presidents really get caught up in this business. They have to support the athletics enterprise. If they don't, they'll lose their jobs." (This is the sad fact about Division I and Division II athletics functioning within the National College Athletic Association in America. This was almost 50 years ago! And it ain't got better since then—of that I'm dead sure!)

I soon found that I simply couldn't psychologically, and then physically, bear any more such shenanigans while at this Illinois scene. Yet I hated to give up my position as department head of one of the very top programs in my field. Somehow the whole situation eventually just "got to me..." The next thing I knew, I had a duodenal spasm. I didn't even know what that was! I'd never had anything like an ulcer in my life, although I had known that my father had a sensitive stomach.

Enough of my long-gone, temporary malady! The die had been cast. I had to get out of there! But where was I to go? Eureka! I couldn't believe my good fortune when Dr. Garth Paton, a former student of mine at the University of Western Ontario on staff there at the time, the university that I had left some 13 years ago, called to say that "Western" had decided that it would start a separate faculty (i.e., college) of physical education). So I immediately applied and was eventually accepted for the position as dean! The president with whom I had struggled had since retired; so, "all was forgiven". Hence back I went to Canada where I knew that intercollegiate athletics was truly kept in educational perspective.

I'd best cut out at this point, because in this preface I am now beginning to "intrude upon" a larger story that I want to tell you about in the course of this entire book. I hope you, the reader, will find it interesting and perhaps useful. I say this because the ongoing tale of corruption in university athletics, the continuing sacrifice of children and youths' physical activity and health education program, and the "unfulfilled promise" of America might, should, must conceivably be turned around. It doesn't look like it will happen that way, but "miracles are still thought to happen occasionally…"

Earle Zeigler
2013

# Prologue

The term "modernism" is used typically to describe cultural movements in today's world that were caused by onrushing science, technology, and economic globalization. It is said to have started in the late nineteenth and early twentieth century. Conversely, postmodernism, as variously defined, can be described loosely as an effort by some intelligent and presumably wise people to react against what is happening to this modern world as it "races headlong" toward an indeterminate future.

It can be argued reasonably that America's thrust is still modernistic to the nth degree. To the extent that this is true, I am arguing here conversely that Canada should work to counteract America's value orientation and political/economic stances as the world moves along in the 21st century. I believe that Canada can— and should do this—by adopting a position that might be called "moderate" postmodernism.

Granted that it will be most difficult for Canada to consistently exhibit a different "thrust" than its neighbor to the south. Nevertheless I believe that now is the time for Canada to deliberately create a society characterized by the better elements of what has been termed postmodernism. In fact, I feel Canadians will be forced to grapple with the basic thrust of modernism in the 21st century if they hope to avoid the "twilight" that is descending on "American culture" (Berman, 2000). You, the reader, may well question this stark contradiction of many of the ideas and actions of our our immediate neighbor. However, bear with me, and let us begin.

What is postmodernism? While most philosophers have been "elsewhere engaged" for the past 50 plus years, what has been called postmodernism, and what I believe is poorly defined for the edification of most, has gradually become a substantive factor in broader intellectual circles. I freely admit to have been grumbling about the term "postmodern" for decades. I say this because somehow it too has been used badly as have other philosophic terms such as existentialism, pragmatism, idealism, realism, etc. as they emerged gradually to become common parlance.

In this ongoing process, postmodernism was often used by a minority to challenge prevailing knowledge, and considerably less by the few truly seeking to analyze what was the intent of those who coined the term originally. For example, I am personally not suggesting, as some have, that scientific evidence and empirical reasoning are to be taken with a grain of salt based on someone's subjective reality. Further, if anything is worth saying, I believe it should be said as carefully and understandably as possible. Accordingly, the terms used must be defined, at least tentatively. Otherwise one can't help but think that the speaker (or writer) is either deceitful, a confused person, or has an axe to grind.

If nothing in the world is absolute, and one value is as good as another in a world increasingly threatened with collapse and impending doom, as some say postmodernists claim, then one idea is possibly as good as another in any search to cope with the planet's myriad problems. This caricature of a postmodern world, as one in which we can avoid dealing with the harsh realities facing humankind, is hardly what any rational person might suggest. How can humankind choose to avoid (1) looming environmental disaster, (2) ongoing war because of daily terrorist threats, and (3) hordes of displaced, starving people, many of whom are now victims of conflicts within troubled cultures? Further, as we still occasionally hear said, what rational being would argue that one idea is really as good as another?

What then is humankind to do in the face of the present confusion and conflicted assertions about postmodernism from several quarters that have been circulated? First, I think we need to analyze the world situation carefully. Perhaps this will provide us with a snapshot of the milieu where we can at least see the need for a changing (or changed) perspective that would cause humankind to abandon the eventual, destructive elements of modernism that threaten us. An initial look at some of the developments of the second half of the twentieth century may provide a perspective from which to judge the situation. Some argue that Nietzsche's nihilistic philosophy of being, knowledge, and morality supports the basic dichotomy espoused by the philosophy of being in the post-modernistic position. I can understand at once, therefore, why this meets with strong opposition by those whose thought has been supported by traditional theocentrism.

It can be argued, also, that many in democracies under girded by the various rights being propounded (e.g., individual freedom, privacy) have come to believe that they require a supportive "liberal consensus" against those who challenge such freedoms whenever the opportunity arises (e.g., the War Against Terrorism). Yet, conservative, essentialist elements in society functioning in democratic political systems feel that the deeper foundation justifying this claim of a (required) liberal consensus has been never been fully rationalized (i.e., keeping their more authoritative orientations in mind, of course). The theoretical foundation supporting a more humanistic, pragmatic, liberal consensus, as I understand it, is called postmodernism by some.

Post-modernists evidently subscribe to a humanistic, anthropocentric belief as opposed to the traditional theocentric position. If so, they would subscribe, also I believe, to what Berelson and Steiner in the mid-1960s postulated as a behavioral science image of man and woman. This view characterized the human as a creature continuously adapting reality to his or her own ends.

Thus, the authority of theological positions, dogmas, ideologies, and some "scientific infallibilism" is severely challenged. A moderate post-modernist— holding a position I feel able to subscribe to once I am able to bring it into focus— would at least listen to what the "authority" had written or postulated before automatically criticizing or rejecting it. A strong post-modernist would go his or her own way by early, almost automatic, rejection of tradition. Such a person appears to be relying on a personal interpretation and subsequent diagnosis to muster the authority to challenge any or all icons or "lesser gods" extant in society.

If the above is reasonably accurate, it would seem that a post-modernist might well feel more comfortable by seeking to achieve personal goals through a modified or semi-postmodernistic position as opposed to the traditional stifling position of "essentialistic", theological realists or idealists. Such a more pragmatic "value-is-that-which-is proven-through-experience" orientation leaves the future open-ended.

The hope would be that postmodern scholars, realizing this increasingly evident rejection of what we might call the "modern ideals," would relate their postmodernism to the emergence of a new, distinct period in the developed countries of the world. The developing countries, seeing this increasingly global, decentralized world society as open, fluid, and emergent, would move to join in at every opportunity. This would become a world in which traditions are being overthrown as new structures emerge because of obvious economic and technological changes that are literally creating a new culture.

## Speculation About the Future

The world continues its evolutional processes. Those who have studied the past with high degrees of intelligence and diligence have offered us a variety of philosophies about humans' history on what we call Earth. It would seem inaccurate, or at least excessive narrowness of definition, to deny any degree of scientific status to the discipline of history. We can indeed argue that with each succeeding generation the study of history, broadly defined, is becoming more of a science, as that term is generally understood.

We can't be sure about what the future holds for humankind, but-if the study of the past is credible-we can surmise that there will be continuing uncertainty. In defense of such a condition, we can argue that uncertainty is both dynamic and stimulating as it concomitantly provides a challenge to us all. What should concern us also is the amount of individual freedom we are permitted living within a type of political state known as a democracy. We still have to prove that democracy is possible over a period of centuries. The prevailing trend toward an increasing number of full-time politicians and an overwhelming percentage of indifferent citizens does not bode well for the future.

The various political communities in the Western world that are democratic political states must stress the concept of political involvement to their citizens and promote this ideal whenever and wherever possible to so-called Third World countries as they become ready to make a choice. In addition to reviving and reconstructing the challenge to people within these countries, we must continue to work for the common good-for freedom, justice, and equality-for people all over the world who aspire to better lives for themselves and their children.

If people learn to live with each other in relative peace, the world may not see devastating nuclear warfare with its inevitable results. As McNeill (1963) stated, "The sword of Damocles may therefore hang over humanity indefinitely" (p. 804). However, it could be that the West and the East will no longer be reacting angrily to each other by C.E. 5000. Perhaps the world may be united into a single civilization through the agency of religion, although the prospects for such a future are remote at present. Toynbee suggests this in his belief that religions may be the "intelligible field" of historical study rather than the investigation of civilizations.

A seemingly better approach could well be the search for consensual values, values that are delineated but free from the strictures of narrow and often dogmatic formalized religions. McNeill looks for "worldwide cosmopolitanism" and "a vastly greater stability" (p. 806).

No matter what we may believe about these conjectures, there is every likelihood that the goal is still a long distance away-especially if a nuclear holocaust is avoided. After all, Earth is *only* about 4 billion years old. According to Sir James Jeans' calculation for the habitability of this planet, men and women, having survived at the rate of 21 civilizations in 6,000 years, still have 1,743 million civilizations ahead of them.

## PART I

# The World and America

## Introduction

Most North Americans do not fully comprehend that their unique position in the history of the world's development will in all probability change radically in the 21st century. For that matter, the years ahead are really going to be difficult ones for all of the world's citizens. The United States, as the one major nuclear power, has assumed the ongoing, massive problem of maintaining large-scale peace. Of course, a variety of countries, both large and small, may or may not have nuclear arms capability as well. That is what is so worrisome.

Additionally, all of the world will be facing increasingly severe ecological problems, not to mention the ebbs and flows of an energy crisis. Generally, also, there is a worldwide nutritional problem, as well as an ongoing situation where the rising expectations of the underdeveloped nations, including their staggering debt (and ours!), will somehow have to be met. These are just a few of the major concerns looming on the horizon.

Indeed, although it is seemingly more obvious with the United States than Canada, history is going against Americans in several ways. This means that their previous optimism must be tempered to shake them loose from delusions about their "historical superiority" they have acquired. For example, despite the presence of the United Nations, the United States has persisted in envisioning itself—the world superpower!—as almost being endowed by the Creator to make all crucial political decisions. Such decisions, often to act unilaterally with the hoped-for, but belated sanction of the United Nations, have resulted in United States-led incursions in the Middle East in Iraq, Afghanistan—you name it!—for very different reasons. And there are other similar situations that are now history (e.g., Somalis, Cuba, the former Yugoslavia, Rwanda, Sudan, Haiti, respectively, not to mention other suspected incursions).

Nevertheless, there is reason to expect selected American retrenchment brought on by its excessive world involvement and overwhelming debt. Of course, any such retrenchment would inevitably lead to a decline in the economic and military influence of the United States. But who can argue logically that the present uneasy balance of power is a healthy situation looking to the future? Norman Cousins appeared to have sounded just the right note more than a generation ago when he stated: "the most important factor in the complex equation of the future is the way the human mind responds to crisis" (1974, 6-7). The world culture as we know it must obviously respond adequately to the many challenges with which it is being confronted presently. The societies and nations must individually and collectively respond positively, intelligently, and strongly if humanity as we have known it is to survive.

## Significant Developments Have "Transformed Our Lives"

In this discussion of national and international developments, with an eye to achieving some historical perspective on the subject, we should also keep in mind the specific developments in the last quarter of the 20th century. For example, Naisbitt (1982) outlined the "ten new directions that are transforming our lives," as well as the "megatrends" insofar as women's evolving role in societal structure (Aburdene & Naisbitt, 1992). Here I am referring to:

(1)  the concepts of the information society and the Internet,

(2)  "high tech/high touch,"

(3)  the shift to world economy,

(4)  the need to shift to long-term thinking in regard to ecology, (5) the move toward organizational decentralization,

(6)  the trend toward self-help,

(7)   the ongoing discussion of the wisdom of participatory democracy as opposed to representative democracy,

(8)   a shift toward networking,

(9)   a reconsideration of the "north-south"orientation, and

(10)  the viewing of decisions as "multiple option" instead of "either/or." Add to this the ever-increasing, lifelong involvement of women in the workplace, politics, sports, organized religion, and social activism, Now we begin to understand that a new world order has descended upon us as we begin the 21st century.

Moving ahead in time slightly beyond Naisbitt's first set of *Megatrends,* a second list of 10 issues facing political leaders was highlighted as "Ten events that shook the world between 1984 and 1994" (*Utne Reader,* 1994, pp. 58-74). Consider the following:

(1)   the fall of communism and the continuing rise of nationalism,

(2)   the environmental crisis and the Green movement, (3) the **AIDS** epidemic and the "gay response,"

(4)   continuing wars and the peace movement, (5) the gender war,

(6)   religion and racial tension,

(7)   the concept of "West meets East" and resultant implications,

(8)   the "Baby Boomers" came of age and "Generation X" has started to worry and complain because of declining expectation levels,

(9)   the whole idea of globalism and international markets, and

(10) the computer revolution and the specter of Internet.

## The World Has Three Major Trading Blocks

Concurrent with the above developments, to help cope with such change the world's "economic manageability" may have been helped by its division into three major trading blocs: (1) the Pacific Rim dominated by Japan, (2) the European Community very heavily influenced by Germany, and (3) North America domi-nated by the United States of America. While this appears to be true to some observers, interestingly perhaps something even more fundamental has occurred. Succinctly put, world politics seems to be "entering a new phase in which the fundamental source of conflict will be neither ideological nor economic." In the place of these, Samuel P. Huntington, of Harvard's Institute for Strategic Studies, believed at the end of the 20th century that now the major conflicts in the world will actually be clashes between different groups of civilizations espousing fundamentally different cultures (*The New York Times*, June 6, 1993, E19).

These clashes, Huntington states, represent a distinct shift away from viewing the world as being composed of first, second, and third worlds as was the case during the cold war. Thus, Huntington is arguing that in the 21st century the world will return to a pattern of development evident several hundred years ago in which civilizations will actually rise and fall. (Interestingly, this is exactly what the late Arnold Toynbee postulated in his earlier famous theory of history development.)

Thus, internationally, with the historical dissolution of the Union of Soviet Socialist Republics (USSR), Russia and the remaining communist regimes are being severely challenged as they seek to convert to more of a capitalistic economic system. Additionally, a number of other multinational countries have either broken up, or are showing signs of potential breakups (e.g., Yugoslavia, China, Canada). Further, the evidence points to the strong possibility that the developing nations are becoming ever poorer and more destitute with burgeoning populations and widespread starvation setting in.

Further, Western Europe is facing a demographic time bomb even more than the United States because of the influx of refugees from African and Islamic countries, not to mention refugees from countries of the former Soviet Union. It appears further that the European Community will be inclined to appease Islam's demands. However, the multinational nature of the European Community will tend to bring on economic protectionism to insulate its economy against the rising costs of prevailing socialist legislation.

Still further, there is some evidence that Radical Islam, along with Communist China, will become increasingly aggressive toward the Western culture of Europe and North America. At present, Islam gives evidence of replacing Marxism as the world's main ideology of confrontation. For example, Islam is dedicated to regaining control of Jerusalem and to force Israel to give up control of land occupied earlier to provide a buffer zone against Arab aggressors. (Also, China has been arming certain Arab nations. But how can we be too critical in this regard when we recall that America has also armed selected countries in the past [and present?] when such support was deemed in its interest?)

As Hong Kong is absorbed into Communist China, further political problems seem inevitable in the Far East as well. Although North Korea is facing agricultural problems, there is the possibility (probability?) of the building of nuclear bombs there. (Further, there is the ever-present fear worldwide that small nations and terrorists will somehow get nuclear weapons too.) A growing Japanese assertiveness in Asian and world affairs also seemed inevitable even though its typically very strong financial position has abated temporarily. The flow of foreign capital from Japan into North America has slowed down somewhat because Japan is being confronted with its own financial crisis caused by inflated real estate and market values. There would obviously be a strong reaction to any fall in living standards in this tightly knit society. Interestingly, still further, the famed Japanese work ethic has become somewhat tarnished by the growing attraction of leisure opportunities.

The situation in Africa has become increasingly grim because the countries south of the Sahara Desert (that is, the dividing line between black Africa and the Arab world) experienced extremely bad economic performance in the past two decades). This social influence has brought to a halt much of the continental effort leading to political liberalization while at the same time exacerbating traditional ethnic rivalries. This economic problem has accordingly forced governmental cutbacks in many of the countries because of the pressures brought to bear by the financial institutions of the Western world that have been underwriting much of the development. The poor are therefore getting poorer, and health (AIDs!) and education standards have in many instances deteriorated even lower than they were previously.

## The Impact of Negative Social Forces Has Increased.

Now, shifting the focus of this discussion from the problems of an unsettled "Global Village" back to the problem of "living the good life" in the 21st century in North America, we are finding that the human recreational experience will have to be earned typically within a society whose very structure has been modified.

For example, (1) the concept of the traditional family structure has been strongly challenged by a variety of social forces (e.g., economics, divorce rate); (2) many single people are finding that they must work longer hours; and (3) many families need more than one breadwinner just to make ends meet. Also, the idea of a steady surplus economy may have vanished, temporarily it is hoped, in the presence of a substantive drive to reduce a budgetary deficit that actually seems insuperable no matter how it is envisioned. The taxation structure in America may have to "take more from the rich," while also not necessarily "reimbursing" the less-advantaged half of the society. It is obvious that major cutbacks are needed in so-called nonessentials while the infrastructure needs reinforcement literally and figuratively.

## Megalopolis Living Problems Are Far From Being Solved

Additionally, many of the same problems of megalopolis living described as early as the 1960s still prevail and are even increasing (e.g., ongoing crime rates, transportation gridlocks, overcrowded schools). Looking northward, in 1967, interestingly, Prime Minister Lester Pearson asked Canadians to improve "the quality of Canadian life" as Canada celebrated her 100th anniversary as a confederation. And still today, despite all of Canada's current identity problems with multiculturalism, she can take some pride in the fact that Canada has on occasion been proclaimed as the best place on earth to live. At the same time, however, the United States has been sliding down the scale in relation to its "international ranking".

Nevertheless, we can't escape the fact that the workweek is not getting shorter and shorter. Also, Michael's earlier prediction about four different types of leisure class still seems a distant dream for the large majority of people. Further, the situation has developed in such a way that the presently maturing generation, so- called Generation Y, is finding that fewer good-paying jobs are available and the average annual income is declining (especially if we keep a steadily rising cost of living in mind). What caused this to happen? This is not a simple question to answer. For one thing, despite the rosy picture envisioned a generation ago, one in which we were supposedly entering a new stage for humankind, we are unable today to cope adequately with the multitude of problems that have developed. This situation is true whether inner city, suburbia, exurbia, or small-town living are concerned. Transportation jams and gridlock, for example, are occurring daily as public transportation struggles to meet rising demand for economical transport within the framework of developing megalopolises.

Certainly, megalopolis living trends have not abated and will probably not do so in the predictable future. More and more families, where that unit is still present, need two breadwinners just to survive. Interest rates, although minor cuts are made when economic slowdowns occur, remain quite high. This discourages many people from home ownership. Pollution of air and water continues despite efforts of many to change the present course of development. High-wage industries seem to be "heading south" in search of places where lower wages can be paid. Also, all sorts of crime are still present in our society, a goodly portion of it seemingly brought about by unemployment and rising debt at all levels from the individual to the federal government. The rise in youth crime is especially disturbing. In this respect, it is fortunate in North America that municipal, private-agency, and public recreation has received continuing financial support from the increasingly burdened taxpayer. Even here, however, there has been a definite trend toward user fees for many services.

## Technology and Life Improvement

By the turn of the twentieth century, "the technocratic idea of progress [had become] a belief in the sufficiency of scientific and technological innovation as the basis for general progress" (Marx, p. 9). This came to mean that if scientific-based technologies were permitted to develop in an unconstrained manner, there would be an automatic improvement in all other aspects of life! What happened—because this theory became coupled with onrushing, unbridled capital-ism—was that the ideal envisioned by Thomas Jefferson in the United States had been turned upside down. Instead of social progress being guided by such values as justice, freedom, and self-fulfillment for all people, rich or poor, these goals of vital interest in a democracy were subjugated to a burgeoning society dominated by supposedly more important *instrumental* or *material* values (i.e., useful or practi-cal ones for advancing a capitalistic system).

So the fundamental question still today is, "which type of values will win out in the long run?" In North America, for example, it seems that a gradually pre-vailing concept of cultural relativism was increasingly discredited as the 1990s witnessed a sharp clash between (1) those who uphold so-called Western cultural values and (2) those who by their presence are dividing the West along a multi-tude of ethnic and racial lines. This multi—ethnicity is occasioning strong efforts to promote fundamental religions and sects—either those present historically or those recently imported legally or illegally—characterized typically by decisive right/wrong morality.

## What Character Do We Seek for People?

Still further, functioning in a world that is steadily becoming a "Global Village," we need to think more seriously than ever before about the character and traits for which we should seek to develop in people. The so-called developed nations can only continue to lead or strive for the proverbial good life if children and young people develop the right attitudes (psychologically speaking) toward (1) education, (2) work, (3) (use of leisure), (4) participation in government, (5) vari-ous types of consumption, and (6) concern for world stability and peace. Make no mistake about it. If we truly desire "the good life," education for the creative and constructive use of leisure—as a significant part of ongoing general education—should have a unique role to play from here on into the indeterminate future.

What are called the Old World countries all seem to have a "character". It is almost something that they take for granted. However, it is questionable whether there is anything that can be called a character in North America (i.e., in the United States, in Canada). Americans were thought earlier to be heterogeneous and individualistic as a people, as opposed to Canadians. But the Canadian culture—whatever that may be today!—has changed quite a bit in recent decades toward multiculturalism—not to mention French-speaking Quebec, of course—as people arrived from many different lands. (Of course, modern Canada was founded by two distinct cultures, the English and the French.)

Shortly after the middle of the twentieth century, Commager (1966), the noted historian, enumerated what he believed were some common denominators in American (i.e., U.S.) character. These, he said, were (1) carelessness; (2) open-handedness, generosity, and hospitality; (3) self-indulgence; (4) sentimentality, and even romanticism; (5) gregariousness; (6) materialism; (7) confidence and self-confidence; (8) complacency, bordering occasionally on arrogance; (9) cultivation of the competitive spirit; (10) indifference to, and exasperation with laws, rules, and regulations; (11) equalitarianism; and (12) resourcefulness (pp. 246-254).

What about Canadian character as opposed to what Commager stated above? To help us in this regard, a generation ago, Lipset (1973) made a perceptive comparison between the two countries. After stating that they probably resemble each other more than any other two countries in the world, he asserted that there seemed to be a rather "consistent pattern of differences between them" (p. 4). He found that certain "special differences" did exist and may be singled out as follows:

Varying origins in their political systems and national identities, varying religious traditions, and varying frontier experiences. In general terms, the value orientations of Canada stem from a counterrevolutionary past, a need to

differentiate itself from the United States, the influence of Monarchical institutions, a dominant Anglican religious tradition, and a less individualistic and more governmentally controlled expansion of the Canadian than of the American frontier (p. 5).

## Postmodernism as an Influence

The orientation and review of selected world, European, North American, regional, and local developments occurring in the final quarter of the 20th century might seem a bit out of place to some who read this book. It could be asked whether this has a relationship to the value system in place in North America. My response to this question is a resounding "Yes." The affirmative answer is correct, also. if we listen to the voices of those in the minority within philosophy who are seeking to practice their profession, or promote their discipline, as if it had some connection to the world as it exists. I am referring here, for example to a philosopher like Richard Rorty (1997). He, as a so-called Neo-pragmatist, exhorts the presently "doomed Left" in North America to join the fray again. Their presumed shame should not be bolstered by a mistaken belief that only those who agree with the Marxist position that capitalism must be eradicated are "true Lefts." Rorty seems truly concerned that philosophy once again become characterized as a "search for wisdom," a search that seeks conscientiously and capably to answer the myriad of questions looming before humankind all over the world.

While most philosophers have been "elsewhere engaged," what has been called postmodernism has become a substantive factor in intellectual circles. I must confess up front that I've been grumbling about—and seeking to grapple with—the term "postmodern" for years. Somehow it has now become as bad (i.e., misunderstood or garbled) as existentialism, pragmatism, idealism, etc.). I confess, also, that I have now acquired a small library on the topic. At any rate, I recently read *Crossing the Postmodern Divide* by Albert Borgman (Chicago, 1992). I was so pleased to find something like this assessment of the situation. I say this because, time and again, I have encountered what I would characterize as gobbledygook describing what has been called "civilization's plight." By that I mean that what I encountered time and again was technical jargon, almost seemingly deliberate obfuscation by people seemingly trying to "fool the public" on this topic. As I see it, if it's worth saying, it must be said carefully and understandably. Otherwise one can't help but think that the writer is a somewhat confused person.

At any rate, in my opinion this effort by Borgman is solid, down-to-earth, and comprehensible up to the final two pages. At the point he veers to Roman Catholicism as the answer to the plight of moderns. It is his right, of course, to state his personal opinion after describing the current situation so accurately.

However, if he could have brought himself to it, or if he had thought it might be possible, I would have preferred it if he had spelled out several alternative, yet still other desirable directions for humankind to consider in the 21st century.

Is this modern epoch or era coming to an end? An epoch approaches closure when many of the fundamental convictions of its advocates are challenged by a substantive minority of the populace. It can be argued that indeed the world is moving into a new epoch as the proponents of postmodernism have been affirming over recent decades. Within such a milieu there are strong indications that all professions are going to have great difficulty crossing this so-called, postmodern gap (chasm, divide, whatever!). Scholars argue that many in democracies, under girded by the various rights being propounded (e.g., individual freedom, privacy), have come to believe that they require a supportive "liberal consensus" within their respective societies.

Post-modernists now form a substantive minority that supports a more humanistic, pragmatic, liberal consensus in society. Within such a milieu there are strong indications that present-day society is going to have difficulty crossing the "designated," postmodern divide. Traditionalists in democratically oriented political systems may not like everything they see in front of them today, but as they look elsewhere they flinch even more. After reviewing where society has been, and where it is now, two more questions need to be answered. Where is society heading? And. most importantly, where should it be heading?

Some argue that Nietzsche's philosophy of being, knowledge, and morality supports the basic dichotomy espoused by the philosophy of being in the post-modernistic position. I can understand at once, therefore, why it meets with opposition by those whose thought has been supported by traditional theocentrism (i.e., in the final analysis, it is God "who calls the shots."). It can be argued, also, that many in democracies undergirded by the various rights being propounded (e.g., individual freedom, privacy) have come to believe—as stated above—that they require a supportive "liberal consensus." However, conservative, essentialist elements functioning in such political systems feel that the deeper foundation justifying this claim of a requisite, liberal consensus has been never been fully rationalized—keeping their more authoritative orientations in mind, of course. The foundation supporting the more humanistic, pragmatic, liberal consensus, as I understand it, is what some people postmodernism.

Postmodernists subscribe largely to a humanistic, anthropocentric belief as opposed to the traditional theocentric position. They would subscribe, therefore, I think, to what Berelson and Steiner in the mid-1960s postulated as a behavioral science image of man and woman. This view characterized the human as a creature continuously adapting reality to his or her own ends (1964).

Thus, the authority of theological positions, dogmas, ideologies, and some "scientific infallibilism" is severely challenged. A moderate postmodernist—holding a position I feel able to subscribe to once I am able to bring it all into focus—would at least listen to what the "authority" had written or said before criticizing or rejecting it. A strong postmodernist goes his or her own way by early, almost automatic, rejection of tradition. Then this person presumably relies on a personal interpretation and subsequent diagnosis to muster the authority to challenge any or all icons or "lesser gods" extant in society.

If the above is reasonably accurate, it would seem that a postmodernist might well feel more comfortable by seeking to achieve personal goals through a modified or semi-postmodernistic position as opposed to the traditional stifling position of essentialistic theological realists or idealists. A more pragmatic "value-is-that-which- is proven-through-experience" orientation leaves the future open-ended.

## What Happened to the Original Enlightenment Ideal?

The achievement of "the good life" for a majority of citizens in the developed nations, a good life that involves a creative and constructive use of leisure as a key part of general education, necessarily implies that a certain type of progress has been made in society. However, we should understand that the chief criterion of progress has undergone a subtle but decisive change since the founding of the United States republic, for example. This development has had a definite influence on Canada and Mexico as well. Such change has been at once a cause and a reflection of the current disenchantment of some with technology. Recall that the late 18th century was a time of political revolution when monarchies, aristocracies, and the ecclesiastical structure were being challenged on a number of fronts in the Western world. Also, the factory system was undergoing significant change at that time. Such industrial development with its greatly improved machinery "coincided with the formulation and diffusion of the modern Enlightenment idea of history as a record of progress…" (Marx, 1990, p. 5).

Thus, this "new scientific knowledge and accompanying technological power was expected to make possible and practical a comprehensive improvement in all of the conditions of life—social, political, moral, and intellectual as well as material." This idea did indeed slowly take hold and eventually "became the fulcrum of the dominant American world view" (Marx, p. 5). By 1850, however, with the rapid growth of the United States especially, the idea of progress was already being dissociated from the Enlightenment vision of political and social liberation.

## PART II

# Life Before the Illinois Scandal

### My "Beginning" in New York City

Born in 1919 at the end of World War I in East Elmhurst, a political entity within the Borough of Queens, Long Island (a borough of New York City), I grew up in what has subsequently become viewed as the "roaring twenties." This "uproar and bedlam" did not really affect me in any significant way, however. At that point I could barely "squeak" underneath the "roar." My mother had divorced my father for infidelity when I was two years old. This was considered a very significant "fracture" in that period. As a tiny tot, of course, I knew nothing about it all.

My mother had a good, mezzo-soprano singing voice. Her brother, my Uncle Louis, played piano well and sang, also. "Somewhere" in a cardboard box, I have a beautiful, color photo of them as a duo playing and singing as semiprofessionals. In the early 1920s, my mother obtained a position at the Adoniram Judson Memorial Baptist Church in lower Manhattan as musical director. (There were other Baptist churches named after this famous missionary who served in India.) She was the choir director and soloist at this church located close to the now infamous World Trade Center site.

As it turned out, when as an adult I eventually got to meet my father, I was 28 years old. I was the only child of the marriage related to that divorce mentioned above. This happened in 1948, just about the time we were moving to Canada the first time. A wrestler on the Yale freshman team I was coaching at the time came from that area on Long Island, NY where I thought my father lived. So, because we were moving away, Bert and I thought we should take this opportunity to look him up—possibly the last chance I would ever get to even know what that "villain" looked like! It was then that I learned that I had a half brother, and that he had gotten "stuck" with the name "Clarence"—one that my mother had rejected for me! (He always called himself "Skip", because he hated his assigned name.) The only one time I had seen my father before then was when my mother took him to court for back alimony payments. I didn't know what it was all about, of course, since I was six years old! We didn't get a chance to speak then... I did see him sitting there in the front row when my mother was called to the witness stand. The lawyer had previously prompted me to follow her closely when she was called—as if we were joined at the hip! I'm sure the judge was impressed.

Evidently, as I learned later also, my grandfather (Conrad) had driven his son, my Uncle Louis, out of the house for one or more reasons. I think he had probably wanted him to get a steady job and contribute to the "family budget" if he were going to live at home. I gather that my Uncle Lou may have also "gotten in with the wrong crowd," as they used to say, while playing around as a young musician. My grandfather was very strict and had a violent temper when aroused; so, I gather that Uncle Louis "went out the door after one of his explosions." This was most unfortunate, because—although he had subsequently married a very nice, attractive lady named Peggy—his marriage ended badly as well. They had one son, Conrad, my only first cousin. He is retired in South Carolina now after a successful career, and we keep in touch by e-mail regularly. He has a lovely extended family that had a reunion quite recently.

*(Note: I am sad to explain further, that later on in mid-1950s [?] I did get to see Uncle Louis again. By then he was short, slender, middle aged, and sort of "down and out." He had moved back in with his parents in East Elmhurst. What happened, I believe, was that he had been in a terrible automobile accident with a bus. He evidently had suffered a serious head injury that affected his brain. He died soon after that one time I met him...)*

Through the devoted efforts of my grandparents (Conrad and Margaret) and working mother (Margery), I spent my early years happily as I eventually learned a bit more than on which side to butter toast. (I'm quite sure we had "toast" at some point back then, but I do remember absolutely that we only had an "ice-box," not a refrigerator back in "the '20s"...) Most of my childhood activities were informal. My grandfather filled in as best he could for my missing father. He was quite interested in baseball and wanted to make sure that I played right-handed. I remember that he took me to the old Yankee Stadium to see several games. This is how I first became interested in Lou Gehrig and Babe Ruth, two of the famous members of the early Yankee baseball juggernaut.

*Note: This is interesting, because I recall that I made certain that my late son, Don, as a teenager, got to know about the exploits of these two outstanding athletes. This is interesting further, because when photos of each of these men became available through some cereal advertisement, the only picture that I had framed was that of Lou Gehrig! I saw to it that this frame hung prominently in my son's bedroom. Why did I do this, especially since Babe Ruth has since been voted the outstanding athlete of the twentieth century? Lou Gehrig, conversely, whose picture I did hang in Don's room was only rated 39th in that particular survey. The answer to this question has a lot to do with why I ended up in Canada. For the answer I urge you, my reader, to turn to the second selection in this book's Epilogue (see p. 149 et ff.)*

Grandmother Margaret, who happened to be left-handed, wanted to make sure that I was left-handed too. She figured that "handedness" was an inherited trait. (My son, Don, is left handed, also,) So, you guessed it, each grandparent bought me a baseball glove for the "correct" hand. Wearing both of them made it a little difficult to throw a ball, but eventually I learned reasonably well. Eventually I did actually throw a ball left-handed. However, in the process I somehow wrote right-handed and played table tennis that way too. I can report further that my career in baseball was rather short-lived, because I was quite nearsighted. (I don't remember when I first acquired eyeglasses. Age 10 or 11?) I often wondered where the ball was, or instead noticed it a bit too late. Becoming significantly ambidextrous did help me in playing handball as an adult, however.

*Note: I learned quite a bit later that the 1920s had been an interest- ing period historically, a fact that I, as a child, of course, didn't ap- preciate. All I can remember,* *for example, is a mental picture of the house my grandparents owned and the surrounding neighborhood. This modest house—then worth about $2,400—has been converted to a day-care facility valued today at about $650,000! Interestingly, fur- ther, when the stock market crashed in 1929, my grandfather lost just about $2,400 on stocks that he had evidently bought "on margin"! Just picture losing the equivalent of the value of your paid-up home over night, so to speak! Shocking...*

### The Move to Connecticut *and a New Name!*

When I was 11 years old, my attractive, talented mother (Margery) married again, this time to a somewhat younger, hard-working, well-intentioned, conservative Baptist minister named James Nelson Zeigler. We three moved to South Norwalk, CT where he was engaged as pastor of the Norwalk Baptist Church. My mother wasn't officially hired too, but she was especially important to the work of the church as choir director and soloist. So, at 12 years of age I had acquired a stepfather and, in a minor way, I suppose you could say that was the start of a normal adolescent life. However, it was also the beginning of my "time of troubles." (Coincidentally, I went almost overnight from being Earle Mattison Shinkle to Earle Zeigler... The town clerk, a member of my stepfather's church, simply issued a most brief statement saying that "henceforth Earle Mattison Shinkle will be known as Earle Zeigler." I still have that piece of paper today in a safe—just in case some technical problem arises for my wife or members of my family when I die.)

*Note: I confess to experimenting with my name after I decided initial- ly on a career as a German teacher and coach. I settled on a middle name of Friedrich! However, E. Friedrich Zeigler—as a German major later at Bates College—eventually just used the middle initial "F".) As I write these words, I am still Earle F. Zeigler and will eventually be buried with that name!*

Reflecting on my youth as a "minister's son", I must admit that back then in 1930 I must have been a "handful" for a fresh-out-of-seminary preacher. The Reverend James N. (Zeigler) was a tall, lanky young Baptist minister at that point who presumed to know the answers to "most everything". "Chaplain Jim"—as he became later for a brief period during WWII—had good intentions, and he actually did his best to cope with me. I was "part of the bargain" when he married my mother, and he certainly never complained to me about the fact of my presence. However, we were *never* on the same wavelength, another fact that indeed helped me decide where I stood on innumerable aspects of life. I should be thankful, however, because such a relationship while an adolescent-as the minister's son-coupled with the developing social and political scene of the 1930s-did a great deal to shape my future orientation to the world around me. In addition, I might not have ever got to attend college if my mother had not remarried. Who knows? Certainly, if I had remained with my father, I might have ended up in some military academy to conclude my education-as did my half-brother "Skip", a moniker he much preferred to his given name of Clarence!

## The "Great Depression Years"

These years comprised the period known as The Great Depression, but that fact really didn't really sink in on me as a young "teenager". Beginning ministers, fresh out of seminary, didn't make much money, despite the fact that my mother's ongoing efforts as choir director and soloist were part of "the total package". However, the position did come with a rather stately old parsonage located at 57 Flaxhill Rd. in South Norwalk, Connecticut. It was a big, old house, as I recall, with a large space for my mother's garden out back. I had my own room with a desk that I don't recall using very much… A baby grand piano took up a good bit of the space in the living room, but there was a sitting room also just as you entered "the parsonage"

I was just beginning get interested in organized sports in junior high school. I played all kinds of childhood sports and games including a bit of table tennis, but, as I recall, I didn't particularly excel at any. For example, I was about 10 years old back in Queens when I started to learn how to swim next to a sewer pipe jutting out into Flushing Bay (an appropriate name for that body of water!). As I recall, the breaststroke was most appropriate in that situation. That waterfront area where I started to "swim" is now LaGuardia Airport named after the famous mayor "Fiorello" of New York City who used to read the Sunday "comics" on the radio for children! . Somehow I also went several times to the YMCA in Flushing,

New York for a swimming lesson. (Interestingly, 15 yrs. later in 1942. I actually served as coach of the YMCA team from Bridgeport, Connecticut that—to my surprise—beat the Flushing YMCA team for the tri-state swimming championship of New York, Connecticut, and New Jersey.)

While attending the Benjamin Franklin Junior High School in South Norwalk, CT, I encountered a bugle. I recall trying out for the Fife, Drum and Bugle Corps—a very brief encounter as I recall. We don't have too many of those around anymore! I can still see that old bugle as it got tarnished and battered. Actually I never *really* learned how to play it... I also took part in a school play that had a "whodunit?" sort of plot. I played the leading role of the detective who uncovered the villain at the end of the play. I recall saying "Aha" as I uncovered the "evil intentions" of the play's villain...

I remember further playing a selection on the piano for a school assembly. I was so nervous that I made an awful mess of it. I suppose even experienced people get nervous on a first occasion like that, and I can rationalize that it was my "first time out..." I was supposed to practice the piano for an hour each day to prepare for my weekly lesson with the very nice, grey-haired church organist by the name of Clarence Cable. However, I was always pushing the hands of the clock ahead during daily practice sessions, wanting to get out and become involved in other activities with friends. (Looking back, I wish I had pushed those clock hands in the other direction...)

I never got to join the Boy Scouts (thank goodness!), or any such organizations, but I did get involved with the YMCA again in high school as soon as I moved to Norwalk, CT. That was the beginning of a 45-year mostly non-professional and highly satisfactory relationship with the YMCA. I'm very sad that the whole character of the YMCA seems to have changed nowadays. It was very helpful to many youngsters at that time, sort of "a home away from home." Now, at least in my community, it's a physical, social and perhaps a bit of an intellectual recreation club for the middle class. Today I believe the Boys and Girls Clubs of America are performing this service that the "Y" provided extremely well for me during my high school days. .

It's important (to me anyhow) to note that even back in the 1920s, in Public School 127 in the Borough of Queens on Long Island, New York City, we had organized elementary school physical education classes. The instruction was formalized, and classes were regularly scheduled. I can't say that I remember being thrilled by the experience, and I can't even remember what happened typically during those periods. I do recall later that in junior high school there was a supply of light wooden dumbbells on wall racks in the gym. Our instructor, Mr. Bean, was quite "military" in his approach and used to walk around calling out instructions with a dumbbell in his right hand. One day, when a difficult pupil irritated him a bit more than usual, he "let fly" with the dumbbell in the general direction of the youngster and accidentally hit him in the head! You can be sure that "Confusion prevailed," but I don't have a clue about the aftermath of that incident.

As a youngster, I had interests in a variety of sports. This interest continued through junior high school, high school, and college. However, I must state again that my memory of the actual physical education classes in a gymnasium at any stage of my education almost completely fails me. This may provide a clue as to their quality… They were certainly not made interesting to me as a youngster, or in high school either. I can remember learning a little bit about how to tap dance in elementary school. This is interesting about physical education history within elementary schools considering that we're talking about the late 1920s and the early 1930s in the Borough of Queens in New York City.

Interestingly, also, I remember that two of my elementary school classroom teachers were Blacks (one man, Mr. Archibald, and one woman (name?). Mr. Archibald was a good teacher and very strict too. He threw the occasional book at "sassy kids," but his aim was better than that of Mr. Bean. He missed purposely; Mr. Bean hit accidentally…

## High School in Norwalk, CT

In that final year of high school, one of my best friends (Gordon Jakob) was elected president of the student council, and somehow in the process I got elected vice president. (Gordon's father was superintendent of schools at that point.) As a "running guard" and "defensive tackle", I was co-captain of the football team in my senior year. In track I ran the 100-yd. dash fairly well and was on the relay team too in my junior and senior years. In my senior year, I won the Norwalk, Connecticut table-tennis championship before heading off to college. I also swam on the YMCA team and won several Connecticut and city free-style and back-stroke sprint swimming championships.

I recall further a variety of events connected with being the stepson of a Baptist minister. One summer when I was in high school, I went away to a youth assembly at the University of Connecticut, Storrs for a couple of weeks and was elected president of that group at some point. I won the sprint races in track & field and in swimming, as well as an underwater swim for distance! (They don't hold that dangerous, breath-holding event anymore...)

I remember also one incident while there when three fellows and three girls stayed out beyond curfew. On the following day, the girls were brought in front of the previously elected "disciplinary" committee! As "president," I was chairing the meeting that was supposed to decide their "punishment." The only problem was that I was one of the fellows who had kept them out! It was the silliest situation ever...

## Bates College "Rah, Rah"! (1936-40)

Somehow or other, it was decided for me—as I recall—that I should go to a private liberal arts college. Colby College in Maine was considered, because it had some sort of a Baptist orientation historically. (My future wife, Bert Bell—as I later learned—was planning to go to the University of Maine. However, at the last minute we both ended up as frosh at Bates College in Lewiston, Maine.) There were four institutions in an athletic conference in the state of Maine: Bates College, Bowdoin College, Colby College, and the University of Maine. They played the various sports together, but Maine has since gotten so large that it's now in a different league.

Attending Bowdoin College was out of the question for me, because it was very exclusive and more expensive than Bates. I had to go to a college where I could work my way through. My high school class graduated in February, 1936;

so for the following six months I worked in a Dobbs hat factory in East Norwalk, CT prior to heading off for Lewiston, ME. There I became an all-wise frosh (ha!) at Bates College where I later majored in German, sort of minored in French, and also took quite a bit of history. Bates didn't have a major program in professional physical education. In fact, I didn't know there was such a thing until later. There wasn't even a minor program in physical education available at Bates. It was a liberal arts and science college; so, I guess my field was regarded asa frill! Hence I hadn't thought of becoming a physical education teacher and coach for my life career. (It is interesting, however, that so many of the people in our field eventually entered professional programs of physical education—now often termed "kinesiology"— because of an early interest in sport?)

As I mentioned above, I met my future wife-to-be at Bates; her name was Bertha May Bell. (They used to kid her with "Bertha may not too…) Her father (Hazen Raycroft Bell)) was a potato farmer in Houlton, Maine, a really nice, hard- working man in the so-called "Shiretown" of the county that was 120 mils north of Bangor, Maine bordering New Brunswick, Canada. Bert hated the name Bertha; so, it was always "Bert." Her mother was a well-intentioned, hard-working lady named Maude, a real worrywart—-if I may use that present-day unfamiliar term. I never felt that she truly accepted me despite that fact that I was a minister's son and she was a "God-fearing Lady." As I recall, also, she was a great cook with everything except meat! Both Maude and Hazen "destroyed" more good beef over the years than you can imagine by insuring that it was "very well done"!

I recall an amusing incident about "dear old Maude" that took place once when we arrived at Bert's home after having worked in the same town during summer vacation between our sophomore and junior years at college. It had been a long trip from CT to Houlton, ME in a 1929 Model A Ford that was so "tired" it used crankcase oil that I would cadge at gas stations along he way. Driving up hills at night off the main highways because the car wasn't properly registered, I looked to see if our old buggy was over heating. Somehow in the process I veered of the road and sideswiped a tree! So thereafter, while we were moving along on the road, the poor old buggy had such a wiggle that its already worn-down tires began to disintegrate at a faster pace than normal. The end result was that I had to change and repair flat tires myself some 21 times before we finally arrived at Bert's home in Houlton, Maine. In retrospect…

Luckily we found several "acceptable" tires of the right size when going through a town in New Hampshire early the following morning.) At any rate, this "changing of the tires" had slowed us down so much that we had ended up sleeping only a few hours during the night at the side of the road. What saved the day really was that this "nice man", who just happened to have two satisfactory, replacement tires under his back porch, also sized up the problem and advised me how to solved the "jiggling steering wheel situation" my Model A was experiencing when in "forward mode"! The trusty vehicle had acquired a bent tie road when I glanced off that tree (i.e., the tie rod being that long piece of metal which somehow joins up the front wheels!) All I had to do was put the tie jack under the rod where the bend was, jack it up a bit, and "Eureka"! The rod became straight enough again to proceed in reasonably "non-shaky" style!

Now back momentarily to why I called Maude Bell, Bert's God-fearing mother, the "worrywart". That same day after we finally arrived in Houlton, her mother insisted on taking Bert to the family doctor for an examination! Guess why? I should mention at this point that Bert had a very nice sister, Barbara, who was always a good friend (as sister-in-law) throughout later life. Barbara was a really nice, warm, attractive person with a cheery disposition. She trained in Bangor, Maine to be a beautician and then remained in Houlton as an adult. Bert, conversely, had figured that the only way she could ever get out of town permanently (!) was to go to college somewhere. (I subsequently kept in even closer touch by telephone with Barbara on the other side of the continent after both her husband, Gerry, and my wife, Bert, had passed away.)

During my freshman year, Bert and I had an ancient history course together that met three days a week at 7:40 a.m. (Imagine listening to a lecture on ancient history at that time of day from a dusty, old, balding professor. Egad!). The class members were seated alphabetically. Bert's last name started with a B and mine with a Z; so we always "sort of met" each other at the door as we filed out of class from opposite ends of the room. However, it wasn't until later in our freshman year that we began to date a bit. At that time, also, I had "sort of " a girlfriend in Connecticut whom I'd met at that Baptist summer assembly discussed above. I kept telling this young lady (Kay DeLong) what a great place Bates College was, and guess what? She ended up there the next year too! I almost lost involvement with both of these young women during that opening year and the one following. However, one relationship eventually survived for 57 years of marriage after college graduation until Bert's death!

*Note: The other "girl friend," Kay DeLong later married the son of the track and field coach at Bates. His name was Dick Thompson. At an initiation ceremony for new Varsity Club members in his sopho- more year, he (blindfolded) ran into a brick wall in the college gymna- sium and was seriously injured. That injury came back to haunt him later as he died quite early. This left Kay with three children to raise. She did so somehow by becoming a successful real estate agent.)*

Everything moved along quite well at Bates that first year. I was extremely busy what with the whirl of things including football, swimming, and track in that sequence "season wise." There were no athletic scholarships; so, at various times during the four-year period, I found work for monetary return at all sorts of things like waiting on table at the dining hall, being janitor on my dormitory floor, and delivering the Boston Globe newspaper on campus. In the upper-class years there, I was also proctor in my dormitory and had a job downtown at a Greek restaurant washing dishes from 5:00 p.m. until about 1:00 a.m. one day a week. (That one day's effort somehow got me my main meal for the entire school year…) Also, in my third and fourth years, I was a teaching assistant in the German department correcting papers for one professor (August Buschmann, a really nice man). Overall, I didn't have much time to hang around. College was a very busy time; that's for sure.

However "disaster did strike" in several ways in year #2, my sophomore year. First, I lost my academic scholarship for one semester because my scholastic average dipped slightly below the standard required. Then I suffered a severe knee injury in a football scrimmage between the varsity and the frosh team. I had just been promoted the blocking fullback position on the varsity (first team!) too…

This serious injury was not attended to by immediate surgery due to an "unqualified" medical doctor. He didn't even call for an x-ray that would have shown the destructive damage done. Hence, I was "automatically" out of football and track, but somehow I found that I could continue with the swimming team—a non-weight—bearing sport, I guess. Another difficult situation arose later that year as well. While working on the switchboard at the Central Maine General Hospital in Lewiston three nights a week that fall, one morning I came down with acute appendicitis. You can imagine how that took me "out of action" for a bit.

*(Note: Talking about "disaster" further…! When I made it back to Norwalk for Xmas vacation during that sophomore year, some friends and I went ice—skating. I had "awful" poorly fitting skates and had only skated a couple of times previously. As I sought to stumble over "wavy" ice to get fully onto Long Island Sound, I fell and must have had a slight brain concussion. However, I evidently continued on "awake" as though nothing had happened… And then, the first thing I remember saying to my friends minutes later was: "Look over there to the northeast; something's on fire! "Something" certainly was! It was Pastor Jim's South Norwalk Baptist Church that was ablaze. I didn't know this until I got home to "the Parsonage" and learned that he had "rushed in" valiantly to save the Church Bible!)*

Then, if matters weren't bad enough, "girl-friend trouble" developed as well. I had started to date Bert Bell, my future wife, toward the end of the freshman year and was continuing to do so at the beginning of the sophomore year. However, as mentioned above, that "sort—of " girlfriend from high school days (Kay DeLong), whom I met at that summer assembly mentioned earlier, had also shown up at Bates in the fall of my second year there. Of course, she soon discovered that I was dating Bert Bell too. So, I found it necessary to soon make a choice—as did they. It's a wonder that I didn't "lose out" with *both* of those young ladies…

I remember one amusing but disconcerting instance from that year viewed in today's light. I had asked Kay DeLong to go with me to a special mid-year dance. She accepted, and then I learned that there were "dance cards" to be filled out in advance. What this meant was that a "reasonable" number of "dance segments" could or should be exchanged so that she and I would have different dance partners for the "segment" designated. One friend of mine was a Black named Howard Kenney; so, I arranged an exchange with him and his partner ("Dottie"). He was an excellent dancer, much better than I was; so, I thought she would really enjoy it. However, when I started to explain the "various dance arrangements" to Kay, she said: "Do you expect me to dance with that 'jigaboo'? I was really taken aback, but somehow convinced her that it would be a good experience, and that people would "frown" at any negative reaction by her. I subsequently learned also that Bates, a small college with a Christian heritage (of course!), had a secret admissions' policy for Blacks and Jews... Times have improved, I think...

My personal "situation" scholastically did improve greatly in my junior year, however. Although playing football and running track were "history" for me because of the injured, "unrepaired" knee, I managed to join the cheerleading squad to lend support to the football team. (Cheerleaders weren't as active then as they are today!). Also, I discovered that I could continue with the swimming team, although my kick was obviously not as strong as previously. My "work situation" improved, also, and additionally I finished the academic year with a 92% average. This sharp rise occurred to an extent because I was taking additional subjects in my areas of specialization.

I can't remember anything special about the senior year at Bates College. I was in a variety of activities—too many I'm sure. Bert and I were "going steady", so to speak. I was the proctor (i.e., peace-keeper) in my dormitory (free room!), the janitor on my floor, and also the teaching assistant in the German department. (Bates College helped me to get through with these part-time jobs.) Frank Coffin, later eminent chief judge of the First Circuit Court of Appeal (New England) was my new roommate for that year. In addition, I was co-captain of the college swim team. However, I was not "at ease" with that involvement because the untreated football knee injury two years previously was still a handicap that made my performance suffer.

There was one funny, interesting incident that I recall, however. I was chairman of the senior class day committee, and our group picture was to be taken with all of us wearing caps and gowns. Somehow I forgot to bring my own mortarboard to the rehearsal. So my roommate, Frank Coffin, sat on the far left in the front row of a bleacher as seated for the photo and—as the camera panned the entire group slowly from left to right—he ran around the back of the group and slapped his cap on my head sitting in the front row on the far right... Needless to say the result was a badly slanted mortarboard on my head, and I looked like a real "goofball" with a silly grin in the final picture that was circulated in the yearbook for "historical purposes".

## Graduate School (Herr Zeigler!)

After college graduation in early June of 1940, my plan was to attend Yale graduate school full time looking to obtaining a master's degree in German. My major professor at Bates College, Sammy Harms—a fine teacher, wonderful man, and friend—had warned me that I was going to get a shock when I hit graduate school in German competing with German scholars there. For example, I hadn't had any practice with German conversation—although somehow my pronunciation was good. My grandparents—with whom I lived early on—had insisted that I learn English only, because German was unpopular after World War I! Hence, no German was spoken in my childhood. That was unfortunate, because in graduate school I was in class with people who had either been born in Germany or had spent years there. (I did take a private conversational lesson once a week that year from a native German lady, but was of minimum help only.)

In addition, I also had to work as a full-time waiter nights at a Childs restaurant to support myself. This combination of responsibilities made for an overall, grim experience. And I can add too that my part-time scholarly efforts were not greeted with "solid approval." I was lucky to survive, but did subsequently receive the M.A. degree in June, 1944. By that time I was working enjoyably in the physical education department at Yale and could see a future as a teacher/ coach in physical education, I had also decided that I wanted to shift my emphasis in graduate work toward a Ph.D. in the School of Education. The German Department didn't object...

During that first year after graduation from college, Bert took a job teaching English and French in Bucksport, Maine. (Note: Because of the archaic approach to the teaching of languages then, she couldn't speak French, and I couldn't speak German! And I had majored in it in college, and she had minored in French!) We corresponded during that first year away from Lewiston, but it was touch-and-go whether or not our relationship would continue. Somehow or other, she came to work in the Connecticut area that summer after graduation, and we began to get more steadily involved with each other again. We then decided to get married on June 25, 1941. The service was performed on a Saturday by my stepfather (Pastor Jim) in the new Norwalk Baptist Church (built after vigorous fund-raising efforts by the parishioners and pastor!). The nuptial occasion was almost marred by the fact that I had to race to Norwalk from New Haven at breakneck speed to reach the marriage license office before it closed at noon!

Immediately after the service and a dinner, and with no "honeymoon", I was slated to become a waterfront lifeguard and swimming instructor at the Madison Beach Club in Madison, Connecticut. I had always wanted to be a lifeguard; sit in a watchtower overlooking the beach; see all the girls in their skimpy bathing suits, wear a pair of white swim trunks, and get a great tan while at the same time receiving a salary! So that summer I became the "bronzed lifeguard" and "valiant swimming instructor." Frankly, it was nowhere nearly the exciting experience I had anticipated. My nearsighted eyes didn't get to see very many "bathing beauties." I had to put Noxema on my nose and wear a sun shield to keep the sun out of my eyes. The "romance" of that setting soon wore off ! It was a boring job, and the water was typically too cold for this "valiant instructor." I was trying to teach shivering children how to swim in Long Island Sound, a body of water whose waves proved quite often that it "had aspirations to become the Atlantic Ocean itself "! (Once on a busy afternoon, with a crowded beach of swimmers of all ages, I launched my rowboat in this surf to "survey my domain" and promptly ended up flat on my face when the sturdy craft hit sand as the wave receded. Talk about embarrassment...)

In addition, Thursday evening was the regular bartender's night off at the Madison Beach Club, CT. Hence I was expected to take his place for several hours. Luckily, folks typically asked for simple-to-make beverages like scotch & soda, rye & ginger ale, a beer, or a glass of wine, or else I would have been "in big trouble". Then, further, I was assigned the task of "bouncer" at the Club's Saturday night dances. Unfortunately it was several years later (!) that I became a "wrestling coach and self-defense expert..." I recall one riotous Saturday night when some drunken guy ran rampant in the Club dining room as dessert was being served. He was fended off somehow by the Greek headwaiter brandishing a chair like a lion tamer, while I managed concurrently to sack his friend coming through an open window to help him by letting loose a right-hand punch... Peace and calm was restored eventually, and representatives from the Madison police department arrived. However, by then the drunken rioter had swum to an island not far off the shore... A wild night...

## My First Position: Y.M.C.A. Secretary

One day in midsummer, the associate secretary for the CT YMCA, who evidently had a summer home near the Madison Beach Club, asked me, "Have you ever thought of working in the YMCA?" I said, "No, but I've had great experiences in the "Y" over the years, and it sounds like a very good idea." He said that there was a fine position open close by, and that I ought to go for an interview to see what might transpire.

It turned out that this was a desirable position for me just starting out as associate physical director and aquatic director at the Bridgeport, CT, YMCA. This was almost "home ground" for me, not very far from Norwalk where I had lived. The starting salary was $1800 a year! So, I began working at the Bridgeport YMCA in the fall of 1941. Luckily I came under the influence of a fine, old, affable physical educator by the name of Harry Abbott. He was a magnificent, aging, but energetic person with a Springfield College background. However, he was very close to retirement and, at the end of my first year, was replaced by Horace ("Red") Smith, a knowledgeable, mature physical educator with a fine athletic background from Cleveland State University in Ohio.

*(Note; my girl friend, Bert had made $1100 as a high school teacher in English and French at Bucksport, ME the previous year. Now, as my wife, she found a job at the local Sikorsky Plant working in the office. For "fitness sake," she decided to ride a bicycle back and forth to work. This was fine until one bright day when a*

*man opened an automobile door in her face! Another disconcerting aspect of this "striving for fitness and transportation" was a fact discovered after a few months of "exceptional physical endeavor" with her "vehicle." She kept saying day after day how hard it was to get the "darned bicycle" up to speed. I figured she was just "getting used to it." We discovered eventually that she had been pedaling the bike with both tires only half inflated…)*

On the job as "associate physical director," I soon realized my deficiency in the whole area of exercise prescription and related physical activity. I had always been involved in team sports, whereas "Y" members typically played all sorts of individual and dual leisure sports. They also wanted to learn "exercise routines". So when someone would say to me, for example, "Hey, come on, let's play some handball." I'd respond that I had to go to work, or give some other lame excuse for not accepting the invitation. I had to decline, because I didn't know how to play handball or badminton, etc. And I didn't want to be a physical director who looked like the proverbial "motor moron".

I decided then and there that I'd better take some more courses in the field in which I had gotten a job, this time to broaden my knowledge of the human body. I hadn't studied basic anatomy or physiology, much less any applied courses of that nature such as body mechanics. What to do? I learned that it would be possible to enroll for some courses leading to what could be called a physical education minor at Arnold College in New Haven, CT in 1942-43.

*Note: Arnold College, a private institution now part of the University of Bridgeport, had been founded in the late 1800s by Ernst Hermann Arnold, a former Turner gymnast from Germany.)*

There I even took a bit of modern dance instruction from Juana de Laban whose father was a famous person in that aspect of dance. These courses were taken part-time while I worked full time at the YMCA on a type of alternating schedule that permitted me to do so. (Actually I completed a few more part-time courses there even after I started working at Yale University in February of 2003.)

## Position #2: Yale University

How I came to work at Yale University is an interesting story. When I started work at the Bridgeport YMCA, I concentrated on what I knew best: swimming and aquatics. I was hired as aquatics director and associate physical director. However, I learned the associate physical director part of the position the hard way (so to speak) by being both diligent and innovative with classes in the gymnasium. Basically, though, I promoted competitive swimming diligently from "Day One" along with the teaching of beginning swimming. Fortunately, in addition, there was an abundance of competitive swimmers around for our competitive swimming team squads, boys and young men who had swum earlier on high school teams.

Soon, needing some competition for the team, I managed to schedule a swim meet against the Yale University freshman swimming team in New Haven (not far from Bridgeport). The director of physical education there was the famous swimming coach, Robert John Herman Kiphuth. (Interestingly, although Mr. Kiphuth at that point was one of the best educated and cultured individuals I had ever met, he could also get "down to earth explicitly" in a matter of seconds. (As it happened, he had never attended any university!) So we swam against Yale's freshman team at a preliminary meet prior to one of their varsity meets. There were some outstanding swimmers on his freshman team, and during World War II years freshmen were also eligible to swim in the varsity meets for upperclassmen.

Mr. Kiphuth didn't want to use his great freshman prospects, his record- holding freshman swimmers, in a "little" meet with the Bridgeport YMCA. Why? Because these freshman were eligible to swim in the immediately following varsity meet with another Ivy League University—and there he thought he was going to really need his "embryonic stars" to win that one! However, the team that I had assembled and trained at odd hours, though many of the team members had not really been "developed" by me, was so good that the overall score was very close right down to the last relay. Kiphuth was a bit upset by this turn of events. Why? He had had to race some of his freshman stars just to beat the unheralded Bridgeport YMCA swimming team, and he had wanted to use them in the varsity meet later that evening.

At any rate, after the meet, Mr. Kiphuth said: "How would you like to work up here at Yale?" His question came out of the blue, and I replied: "Gee, that would be interesting. Thank you. I'd like to think: about it." He said, "Give me a call next week and tell me what you have decided." I vaguely remember making that phone call and subsequently leaving YMCA employment. A man by the name of Howard Haag had recently taken over for "Perly" Foster as the general secretary of the Bridgeport YMCA. When I told him about this chance to go to work at Yale, he said, "This is a serious decision, let us pray!" The next thing I knew he was praying for me right there in his office, even though I didn't exactly have "the greatest relationship with the Northern Baptist Convention." In fact, by that time I was confirmed agnostic!

So, with some "guidance from above," this is how I got to work at Yale where my starting salary in February of 1943 was the magnificent sum of $2400 a year. (Somewhere along the line, they paid me "something extra" for helping to coach football and wrestling, also.) Originally I thought I was going there to work as an assistant to this great swimming coach. As it turned out, however, there were several other fellows waiting in line to be "assistant swimming coaches" too! Because of Kiphuth's fame as a swimming coach, anyone involved in the Yale physical education program also needed some knowledge and/or competency in swimming! With two magnificent pools in the famous Payne Whitney Gymnasium, there was great emphasis on the teaching of swimming, the holding of workouts, officiating at meets, keeping track of records, and the actual running of the swimming meets. Kiphuth's "formidable impact" at Yale was such that every student had to pass a 100-yard swimming test before he could get his "Yale diploma"!

Interestingly, despite all of my previous emphasis on swimming and aquatics, as it developed I became an assistant wrestling coach there instead! (I did teach some swimming classes and assist at swim meets, of course.) One day they needed help on the 6th floor in the Gymnasium. It was during World War II, and with the teaching of combat and self—defense to various members of the armed forces studying there was required along with proficiency in swimming and overall fitness. Mr. Kiphuth, my department head said: "Hey Zeig, they need more help upstairs in the wrestling room." My response was that I had never wrestled; I was a swimmer. "I know that," he said, "But go see Eddie O'Donnell, the coach. They're short handed, and maybe you can learn something and help him and his brother Johnny out for a while."

When I walked in the door of the wrestling room on the sixth floor, I must have looked youthful. Coach Eddie O'Donnell said: "Hello, son. How much do you weigh?" He thought I was a candidate for his wrestling team! I tried to explain lamely that Mr. Kiphuth had sent me up to "help out." This got Coach Eddie on edge. (He was also a private physiotherapist, as well as the trainer for varsity football.) He rushed down to ask Kiphuth what this was all about. I think he thought I was after his job or something… When he returned, I told him I knew nothing (!) about wrestling or self defense, but that maybe I could learn enough to help out a bit. This mollified him, and it was the beginning of a five-year relationship with NCAA amateur wrestling… (Later after leaving Yale, I would telephone Eddie periodically to say "hi!" Actually I called him on the day he was dying, but his wife was so upset that it was a very short conversation with her…) I'd never wrestled, but I learned about it and self-defense fast! This would never happen in this way nowadays.

There are two incidents worth relating about my wrestling and self-defense days at Yale. The first has to do with me learning aspects of self-defense and combat. In between class periods one day, an Air Force cadet with a black belt in judo was showing me how to employ a "break-fall" (i.e., how to land on the mat below when your opponent throws you up in the air over his hip). As part of our practice session, each of us was to throw the other thereby giving the "throwee" a chance to practice slamming his arm on the mat when he landed thereby lessening the impact. On one of his throws I lost track of "where the mat was" and in the process of landing suffered a shoulder separation. (This was known proverbially as a "dropped" shoulder.) Nevertheless I had to continue teaching the self-defense class with my left arm in a sling. This proved to be amusing to a sergeant whom the captain sent up to help me out by the name of Broderick Crawford. "Oldtimers" will remember "Brod" as the burly ("10-4") TV sheriff and famous movie actor. One of the "moves" we had class members practice was called a shoulder roll, and typically the instructor demonstrated it once before asking the class to do the same. Somehow big, and somewhat awkward "Brod" landed incorrectly on his shoulder and ended up with exactly the same injury that I had "acquired"— only his separation was worse. That was the last I ever saw or heard of Sergeant Crawford… He applied for exemption from service because of that injury and reportedly enjoyed a 15% disability pension for the rest of his life—not that he needed a dime of that stipend…

The other incident—as I explained above—has to do with the fact that I, who had gone to work at Yale presumably as an assistant *swimming* coach, ended up with part of my assignment being the freshman *wrestling* coach. I often wondered how I would do as a wrestling competitor! The chance to find out arose in the spring of 1946. This was before—I believe—that I was scheduled for a "belated" right- knee operation. (Recall my "football career—ending accident explained earlier in my second year of college,) The Connecticut State YMCA Championships were scheduled right there in downtown New Haven. So I talked it over with Johnnie O'Donnell, Eddie's younger brother, who was the assistant wrestling coach and had become a good friend. "Why not?" he said, and so I entered this event scheduled for a few month later.

So I started to train by running and practicing with wrestlers that we were coaching. Unfortunately, I hurt my right wrist somehow about a month before the tournament. What to do? All I could do was to continue with my running even more diligently than before. My wrist was "okay" by the weekend of the tournament. Somehow I managed to get through several preliminary matches on the Friday and early Saturday sessions because the competition wasn't too tough. So here I was on Saturday evening in the finals of the tournament in the 155 lb. class. (I had made the 155 lb. limit quite easily by eating carefully for a week or so before.) I said to Johnnie O'Donnell, Eddie's younger brother, who happened to be the match referee: "Who is this fellow I'm wrestling in the finals?" "Oh, don't worry," he said: "he's a "bum." Well, it turned out that this "bum" had won the state title three times previously, and in 1945. the previous year, had won the open 145 lb. title in Hawaii while he was in the armed forces there. These achievements of my opponent were announced just before my match with him started (as if it were a professional boxing match!). Well… The only thing that saved the day for me was that I was basically a little bigger than he was and also quite strong. So the score was even at the end of the official three, three-minute periods—and we went into overtime. I started on top of him on the mat as prescribed for the first of two overtime periods of two minutes each. After a while I could hold him down no longer, but—instead of letting him up to score one point only—I struggled to hold him down and he was able to reverse me and got on top in control. That added two points to his score!

In the second overtime period starting down on the mat, he was in the top position. If I could reverse him, I would earn two points creating a tie. The minute that the referee, my fellow coach (John) at Yale, made the move for us to begin, my opponent stood up ceding me one point. This made it two points to one in his favor. Now it was up to me to "catch up" to him and take him down to the match successfully to earn any points. As it happened, both of us were exhausted. He "ran" (i.e., kept backing up), and I could get a hold of him enough to even try to take him down. The trick at this point is for the wrestler "being chased" to make it look like he really wants to engage with you—even though he really doesn't because he's ahead on points! Frankly, I was so tired that I don't know what I could have done if I had caught him... He had outsmarted me, and I lost 2-1 in overtime. All in all, it was a good experience, and hence I no longer was a wrestling coach who had never wrestled...

## Eyeball Flaw a Determining Factor

The World War II years were disturbing, of course, but proved also to be a very interesting time for me. Why didn't I get drafted for military service? I mentioned earlier that I was nearsighted. In addition, I also had a knee injury that was not x-rayed or operated on when it occurred in the early fall of 1937 (my sophomore year at Bates). However, those two factors would not have caused a deferment. I had another eye problem as well—one I had never really known about or understood. There was a flaw on my left eyeball from birth, perhaps as a result of silver nitrate being put, or not being put, in my eyes (?). Whatever had occurred, the flaw had developed a condition labeled as a constant oscillating nystagmus. That means that my eye is constantly trying to adjust. Why? Simply this: the flaw "tells" my eye that the scenery "out there" isn't lined up correctly. Thus, my head tends to move a tiny bit most of the time. I recall going to an ophthalmologist when I was in high school, and he had said: "Yes, you're going to have difficulty." He knew that I was interested in sports include those that require hand-eye coordination. How could I tell him that I'd won the city table tennis championship just the week before? On the other hand, I think it might have been true that I indeed had been having some difficulty as a result of my eye trouble. I might have been even a better table tennis player without that problem!

When I was studying and working in New Haven in early 1941, I did get the draft call! As it happened, I had previously gone for a second eye examination, and the doctor had said: "This is an interesting case. We don't see very many of these. The nystagmus that you have would disqualify you from service in the armed forces." I'd had a knee injury from football, but I figured that my eyesight couldn't make any difference as far my eligibility for induction into the army was concerned. The word was that, if "they looked in one ear and couldn't see out the other side," they automatically figured you were healthy enough as far as the rest of the body was concerned. However, this doctor insisted, "No, this eye problem is going to keep you out." He said, "My associate and I are the two doctors who check eyes for military—induction physicals. I'm going to write a note to my colleague saying that we can't let you in the service." Half of me was very upset, and the other half was greatly relieved...

Still I was more or less able to soothe my conscience about not being eligible for the service because my position at Yale was partially as a civilian instructor to students and other young men training in this or that branch of the armed forces stationed there. When I began working in the physical education department in early 1943, I also necessarily got involved in corrective physical education and remedial gymnastics. Bob Kiphuth was tremendously interested in that type of experience for young men with bad posture. He had traveled abroad to take seminars with Dr. Bess Mensendieck, a European specialist of the time in remedial work and body mechanics. In fact, at that time all freshmen at Yale had to undergo a body mechanics examination. Somehow I was assigned to corrective physical education work for a couple of hours a day. It did appear to be useful knowledge to acquire, even though this approach was a static sort of postural training experience. In addition, I must report sheepishly that, because of my assignment in self-defense and wrestling, I occasionally practiced a bit of judo and self-defense on my wife to her dismay in order to get practice with some of the skills I was supposed to be teaching the next day in those self-defense classes.

## That's Me "All Over"...

As part of my overall workload, I taught body mechanics, wrestling, hand-to-hand combat, swimming, squash racquets, and warfare aquatics as a physical education instructor. In addition I soon also got a chance to help in the coaching of both football and wrestling. Further, over and above such practical, on-the-job experience at Yale, I was taking a few theory and practice courses in physical education at Arnold College that was still located in New Haven at the time. Still further, I finally completed the master's degree in German at Yale in June of 1944.

Then, starting in September of the 1944-45 academic year, I found an opportunity to teach scientific German part time to potential pharmacists at the New Haven branch of the University of Connecticut. I don't know, in retrospect, how I managed to squeeze it all in... This continued for a four-year period until I left for a post in Canada. (In departing I convinced the dean that these pharmacists-to-be might be better off with a course in salesmanship.) All in all, it truly was a busy time! I often wonder now how I survived it all...

At this time all of the different branches of the armed forces had units at Yale for six, eight, or 10 weeks, three months, or one year. If they had not made such arrangements with America's military program, private institutions such as Yale might have gone out of business because undergraduate enrollment dropped so significantly. Interestingly, however, even the famous Glen Miller and his Army Air Force Band was stationed there. He used to come in and play badminton on the fifth floor of the Payne Whitney Gymnasium. I would mumble "Hi" as he went by. He would smile and nod, but didn't know me from Adam, of course. All together, about 3000 ROTC, ASTP, Air Force and USN people attended without their tuition fees paid for by Uncle Sam. These military people didn't get involved in any of the external competitive sport programs, however. They had their own intramural sports, club groups, and fitness programs. The regular Yale population went on with its intercollegiate athletic program as best it could, but only the Navy enrollees were permitted to take part with them.

In passing, I should mention that I had applied to enter the master's program in physical education at Springfield College part time in the fall of 1944 after I completed my work in German. They said, "Okay, but you need all of these undergraduate prerequisites." There were so many of them to make up that I just didn't see how I could take the time from my full-time employment at Yale to fulfill this demand. So I next applied to Teachers College, Columbia in the upper Bronx of New York City for part-time study. They said: "Fine, come along." When I told them that I didn't have an undergraduate degree in physical education, they replied: "That's all right as long as you have completed any bachelor's degree successfully!" It was ridiculous how easy it was to get into Teachers College—and how difficult it was to get into Springfield College. Of course, I took the line of least resistance for obvious reasons (including mode of transportation available).

*(Note; I eventually spent some time at Springfield College when I was doing my dissertation in its old library uncovering early historical materials. In fact, I discovered that their literature listed the wrong date for the beginning of Springfield College. I informed them, and the registrar subsequently changed it in their bulletin.)*

## Getting That "Union Card": the Ph.D.

By this time in my career, I knew that I wanted—and really had to have—a doctoral degree! This was the situation because it would be required to work and make progress in university circles. So, I was able—fortunately—to enroll in the School of Education right there at Yale and take courses part time toward the Ph.D. degree. The obvious course for me to follow there was specialization in the history and philosophy of education. This was possible even though I'd had only a couple of undergraduate professional education courses at Bates College. My overall "down—to—earth" plan for the future at that point was to teach some German, and also to teach physical education and coach, at a New England preparatory school. I was quite certain that Bob Kiphuth would eventually help me locate a position there, because he had a great relationship with many New England private schools from which he recruited future swimmers.

Then I accidentally learned one day that another reason why Mr. Kiphuth had brought me to Yale was that he hoped to start a small professional preparation program in physical education there. He knew about the early history of the Harvard Summer School in regard to preparing physical education teachers, and he wanted to start something similar at Yale. Additionally, Bob (as he insisted [!] on being called) knew also that many Yale graduates were being hired as young masters at New England preparatory schools. He wanted these young men to have a strong physical education background, because he was a great believer and advocate of exercise and fitness. However, his long—range vision for a program at Yale was limited in the sense that he really didn't expect to be permitted to institute a degree program in physical education. Hence he wanted to have Yale at least offer a couple of professional physical education courses. Obviously, I then realized that he most certainly would never seek to initiate a master's or a Ph.D. program! When I went to enroll in Yale's School of Education part time, I soon discovered that one could not get two master's degrees from the University. I had thought that—even though I already I had one there (i.e., German) that one in education would also be a requirement before starting on a dissertation in the same field. At any rate I actually soon had the equivalent of a master's degree in education as well, and then also successfully completed what are were called the "preliminary examinations". At that point, however, I realized that I still needed some additional background work for a career in physical education. As I mentioned above, I could be admitted; so, I did actually enroll and start working on a master's program at Columbia Teachers College, Columbia in New York City. At the time, Columbia and New York University (NYU) were the two foremost places in eastern America for graduate study in physical education.

The famous Jesse Feiring Williams (famous-that is in my field in the first half of the 20th century), a medical doctor, had been there for decades at Columbia Teachers College. However, he had just retired after some controversy with "higher administration". "The word" was that he had issued an ultimatum to which the "powers that were" evidently didn't accede. As a result, he retired early, and I missed having a course from this "legend" in our field. Clifford L. Brownell, Harry Scott, William L. Hughes, Herbert Walker, Josephine Rathbone, and Hally Poindexter were also there. Josephine Rathbone was one of my first professional instructors with whom I actually studied corrective physical education. (I say this even though one of my assignments at Yale was to actually teach it!)

She had solid knowledge in that area and was a dynamic person who typically "took center stage". In fact, she would have been a success in Hollywood, not necessarily as a glamorous, romantic heroine, but as a character actress. As I look back on it, she was the most impressive person that I encountered at Teachers College. She was also very helpful and nice to me. Hence I was delighted later to be asked to read her memorial statement at the American Academy of Physical Education session. I decided to put an original statement together, because some-one had just passed "something" along to me that Jack Berryman had written for use with the American College of Sports Medicine to which she belonged, also. Hence I read the statement while they showed a nice slide picture of "Jo" Rathbone—"Josephine Rathbone Karpovich", as she liked to be known.

*(Note: Jo had at some point married Dr. Peter Karpovich from Russia. Interestingly, Dr. T. K. Cureton Jr., my colleague at Illinois (UIUC) later, had been at Springfield College as a student earlier, where he studied under him. Later they had perhaps one of the worst conflicts that ever existed between two "personalities" in our field.)*

While taking courses at Teachers College, I had another fine woman instructor by the name of Professor Rose, a well-known nutritionist. As it happened, I would travel by train from New Haven, CT (where Yale is located) down to Columbia University in upper New York City on Friday afternoons, attend one class on Friday evening and another on Saturday morning. Typically I spent those Friday nights after class with my grandparents (Conrad and Margaret Beyerkohler) in borough of Queens on Long Island east of the City where I had been born on August 20,1919.

Given the learning experience in physical education I already had from the courses I'd taken at Teachers College and Arnold College, along with the in-service studying that I had to do to prepare for teaching corrective physical education to Yale freshmen, I soon discovered that I really wasn't learning very much more in Columbia Teachers College master's program. Also, there were many "picky" requirements. For example, there was a required advanced course in administration of physical education and athletics. However, I'd already had one course in administration there, and *they were using the same syllabus at both the undergraduate and graduate levels.* Nevertheless, my academic adviser said, "You have to take that course because it's a requirement." I said, "But you're using the same syllabus all over again." No matter...

Fortunately, by that time I was already working on the doctorate in the Department of Education at Yale; so, I "checked out" of Columbia. I figured that I had completed the equivalent of a graduate minor, and that it would be a waste of time and money to finish the master's degree there. Hence, I ended up with a master's in German, the equivalent of a master's degree in education, and the equivalent of undergraduate and graduate minors in physical and health education at Arnold College and Columbia Teachers College, respectively. The only degree left for me to obtain was the Ph.D.!

Hence, still working full-time in the physical education department "full time" and in the athletics program "part time" at Yale, I started on a part-time basis in the doctoral program in the graduate department of education there. (I don't think one would be permitted to do that today!) Most fortunately, I soon encountered John S. Brubacher, one of the great professional educators of the 20th century. (Actually, he was later chosen by a select committee as one of the 11 great people in the field of professional education through 1975 in the 20th century.) Interestingly, it just so happened that he had an interest in competitive sport, Yale football in particular, and I was an assistant football coach right there!

*(Note: Of course, I had "stumbled" into the position as assistant football coach. One day, while playing handball with then football coach, Howie Odell, as we returned to the locker room, he said: "Hey Zeig, didn't you play football in college?" So, after telling him about my experience both on the line and in the backfield and the resultant knee injury, He said, "Come on out and help us after your work in the gym." So I became assistant line coach for a couple of years, then junior varsity*

*coach, and finally freshman line coach when Odell left and Herman Hickman took over. )*

So, there I was, taking courses in the history of education and the philosophy of education with the eminent John Seiler Brubacher, who subsequently became my doctoral thesis advisor. Of all the teachers I knew in my life, this fine man probably had the greatest influence on me. He was a Yale Phi Beta Kappa and a brilliant person. His teaching approach was excellent, and later I followed through applying his persistent problems approach to the teaching of both the history and philosophy of my own field within education down to the present. At that time, educational philosophy still emphasized a sort of "systems approach" where one drew implications for practice the philosophic positions of realism, idealism, pragmatism, existentialism, and so forth.

*Note: Years after I had completed my degree at Yale and had moved from Western University to work at the University of Michigan in 1956, Dr. Brubacher and I used to play chess every two weeks at the Michigan Union. I never won… Despite these continual losses, these pleasant sessions had been indirectly possible through the courtesy of Yale's president. "One bright day", President Whitney Griswold of Yale had managed to convince his Board of Governors that the School of Education there should be abolished. (Harvard University has its School of Education to the present day). So, Dr. Brubacher was quickly recruited by Dean Willard Olson of Michigan's School of Education.)*

When the time came to pass the required comprehensive examinations for the doctoral degree prior to the writing of a dissertation in Yale's School of Education, I discovered that the education department would also allow a degree candidate to substitute a comprehensive paper covering his or her subject matter. I thought: "With my 'mixed—up' background, maybe I'd be best advised to follow that route." My assigned advisor for the "comps" was Dr. Charles Wilson, an outstanding health educator from Columbia Teachers College who had been hired by Yale. I went to him and said, "Dr. Wilson, I'd like to analyze professional programs in physical education in the Big Ten for my comprehensive project next year" He said, "Okay, why don't you write up a little outline of it." I did, and he agreed to let me go ahead with this analysis. I then spent the entire year in my free time researching and writing about this topic.

About six weeks after I handed in the comprehensive paper in late May of 1948, I received a nice note from Dr. Hill, the chairman, saying, "The paper that you turned in to Dr. Wilson was fine. However, he is new here, and he didn't appreciate fully what our 'comprehensives' consist of—and therefore what your paper actually should have consisted of." I then had an interview to find out just why it wasn't acceptable. Come to find out, the paper should have been a comprehensive analysis of all the different areas *within* professional education (i.e., educational administration, educational psychology, educational curriculum and methodology, education history and philosophy, etc.) My reaction was: "Oh!" Of course, what I was being told made good sense... I can't recall what Dr. Wilson, a nice man, had to say about his misunderstanding—and thus mine as well.

Dr. Hill, who had called me in, then said, "Maybe you can do this comprehensive paper this coming year." There I sat with a thick sheaf of papers that I had spent the entire year researching and writing. Actually I had just met the deadline. I quickly thought that perhaps Columbia Teachers College would accept the paper as a master's thesis. (My adviser didn't yet know that I planned to "bow out" there!) So I asked a number of different professors at Teachers College if he or she would let me work in the area of professional training and, with some revisions, accept my comprehensive physical education paper as a master's thesis.

The Teachers College's catalog actually said that degree candidates could take the thesis or the non-thesis route. However, I couldn't find anyone there to help me on that basis. No one wanted to be bothered... "The word" was simply that students weren't taking the master's—thesis route anymore. As a result, I really did make the final decision to check out of Columbia Teachers College at the end of that summer!

So next I worked away and turned in the required type of comprehensive report at Yale at the end of the subsequent year. In retrospect, I guess that too was a good experience to have "under my belt". Happily, after I struggled with another "tome" and submitted it on time, in August at the end the summer session, I received a note from Dr. Hill saying, "You have now met this requirement, and Dr. Brubacher has agreed to be your major advisor. Take it from here." Whew…

So, early in the new school year, I took a doctoral proposal to him that I then gradually refined based on his advice. My mammoth doctoral study traced the history of professional preparation in physical education in America from 1861 to 1948. I initially wanted to write a world history of physical education, but that would have been far too prodigious an undertaking. So I changed that with the idea of writing only an American history of the field. However, Dr. Brubacher wisely said that such a project was *also* too broad and inclusive. My next proposal was to undertake research as to what might be called an "American philosophy of physical education." Once again, he looked at me, asked me to turn my head to one side, and then said: "You don't have gray hair or sideburns yet; why don't you wait a while before you undertake the writing of "an American philosophy"? By the way," he continued: "Has anyone ever written a history of professional preparation for physical education in the United States?" I went away and checked this idea out, and no one had. This seemed like a manageable topic, but—as it turned out—it too became a most unwieldy, unmanageable topic for the next five years. Nevertheless, for a number of reasons, it became the best possible thesis topic I could ever have undertaken"! An explanation follows…

In my study I divided the history into three parts: 1861 to 1889, 1890 to 1919, and 1920 to 1949. Since it turned out to be such a stupendous task, I had to limit and define wherever possible. I started by writing information on all aspects of our field on index cards. This was long before the day of computer storage; so, I ended up with a raft of card file boxes. On each box I attached a metal file indicator for specific topic identification. I had a blue indicator for physical education, an orange one for health education, etc. It became a horrendous task. After a year of spending every spare moment on that approach, I said to Dr. Brubacher, "I'm not sure how I'm going to bring all of this under control." He said, "Why don't you pick out representative universities and/or colleges of different types, in different parts of the country, and then follow them through from period to period according to the persistent problems approach that I myself use when writing history." (According to his definition, a "problem" was something that was "thrown forward" from era to era.) My reaction was: "Gloryoski"! I then approached the project from that much more manageable standpoint...

Some of the problems or concerns that I dealt with affect all aspects of society: values, the type of political state, the presence of nationalism to a greater or lesser extent, the impact of economics, and the impact of religion. Actually that has been the question I've traced over the centuries (i.e., the extent to which each has influenced my field). (I've subsequently added ecology, science and technology, and the impact of striving for peace to that list.) Although that last topic hasn't yet fully "coagulated," it will in time work its way along to greater status. I am still collecting information in those areas at this time of writing (2012, some 60 yrs. later) as they apply to the overall field of physical activity education (including educational sport). Brubacher himself based much of his own historical work on the impact of "persistent problems" on the overall field of education in this way. (Actually each field within education could have its own set of professional concerns and persistent problems.) I worked up those for my field within education and have since kept track of them down through the years. In fact, I've organized some of my books that way.

In other words, the historical development of the curriculum in physical education is, for example, one persistent problem, and teaching methodology another; the question is how each has changed over the years. Other problems specific to our field were the nature of professional preparation, the administration of programs, the relationship of physical education to highly competitive sports, the concept of progress, the role of minorities, etc. (My mentor, Professor Brubacher, kidded me because I included women as a "persistent problem" in the "minorities group" trying to achieve equal opportunity within the field. We also developed concepts about the use of leisure and about the healthy body.) Basically, therefore, that's the way I went about approaching the history of professional preparation in my field in the United States with my thesis.

As my research progressed, I learned a lot more about Springfield College because it was one of the eight institutions that I studied (based on the earlier delineation my adviser had recommended). I also traced the evolution of the Harvard Summer School until its closure in 1932, as well as that of Eastern Michigan University in Ypsilanti as another of the eight programs selected. I followed each of those eight institutions from era to era in relationship to each of the persistent problems that prevailed with their programs of professional preparation. This organizational arrangement did indeed make the task more manageable. As it evolved, I spent four years of as many nights, weekends and summers as possible on the thesis. The finished manuscript totaled 506 pages, including bibliography. It had indeed been a massive chore! Nevertheless, I really did learn to use Brubacher's problems approach historically, descriptively, and philosophically. In addition, "acquiring this specific understanding" eventually helped me tremendously with the application of the subjects of history and philosophy to my field. This is especially true because at the time both of these courses in our field's professional curriculum was mired down with courses using only (1) a dry, traditional, chronological approach to my field's history with that traditional course, and (2) a so-called "principles" of physical education approach and/or the analysis of the concept of "physical education" in courses related to philosophy of physical education.

## My First Publication

As I explained above, while working at Yale full time, I had started on my doctoral dissertation there, also. In addition, I was still involved with graduate courses at Columbia Teachers College too. In the spring of 1948 there, I wrote a term paper on Sheldon's somatotyping of the human body for Prof. Josephine Rathbone's course. Subsequently the paper came back to me with a handwritten note saying, "See me immediately." I thought: "Uh—oh, what did I do wrong?" I went to her and said. "Dr. Rathbone, you wanted to see me?" She replied: "Zeigler, your paper on somatotyping must be published immediately." She told me to make certain changes and bring it back to her a.s.a.p. She would than send it to the editor of our leading journal (*JOHPER*) and recommend to her that its contents must be made available to the profession immediately. Naturally I did as she had instructed me most willingly. That was how my *first* article, "The Influence of Sheldon's Somatotyping on Physical Education," was published in late 1948. I confess that this was my last experience with somatotyping, because it most certainly wasn't my intended area of specialization. The paper had just been written as a course assignment, and my "strengths" eventually were in history, philosophy, management, international and comparative physical activity education, and professional preparation as applied to my field within public education. At any rate, this is how I got my start with "publication"—my first of what at the moment totals some 445 articles and 57 published books and monographs.

## How I Happened to Move to Canada

In the summer of 1947, as I explained above, I was still taking courses at Teachers College. One evening I stopped to exchange pleasantries with a fellow working at the switchboard at the entrance to Army Hall, our living quarters. As it turned out *(LIFE IS STRANGE!),* this young man was Jack Fairs, an instructor and backfield football coach at The University of Western Ontario. He was filling in for his dormitory roommate for two hours at the switchboard that night—*and never worked there again!* My timing was perfect! We became friends, and a week or so later he asked: "Would you consider coming up to Canada for a job interview?" So I went for an interview at Western Ontario University (now Western University).  Actually my wife didn't even go along with me. We had our little boy, Don, by then, and daughter Barbara was on the way. It didn't make much sense for *all* of us to make the trip, because we weren't sure that we wanted to leave America anyhow. After I arrived, met several people, and considered the possibilities of the situation there at "Western", they shortly offered me a position that would turn into a department headship as a full professor when the doctoral degree was granted. You can imagine Bert's consternation when I returned home to Connecticut—and she hadn't even seen the place! I must give her full credit (!) for taking my word that it was a "fine opportunity…"

However, immediately upon arrival there in London, Ontario, Canada, I began to understand that—if I were to become department head—they were going to have to get busy with the firing of the man who only several years before had filled that position. Earlier I had gone to Prof. Harry Scott, who was at Teachers College at the time, and told him I wanted to talk to him confidentially. I said:

"Dr. Scott, this is the situation." Scott's response had been: "Why don't you stall your move for a year. Maybe the situation will resolve itself so that you won't be stepping into a situation where they're trying to get rid of a department head." Hence, I had indeed talked them into waiting for a year by using the excuse that I was just finishing up my doctoral dissertation.)

In the meantime, I was indeed still working along on my exceptionally long dissertation. (Actually I didn't finally get the degree until February, 1951, a year and a half after I arrived at Western.) I didn't know that the department head at Western Ontario, whom I would replace, was Harry Scott's advisee, and that Harry—my Columbia professor—was torn two ways by the situation. Evidently, Scott did finally ask this man confidentially: "Do you know that they're planning to get rid of you and bring in Zeigler as department head?" As you can imagine, this chap wasn't exactly thrilled by my impending arrival to campus. (Also, I wasn't thrilled either that Scott had broken confidence with me!)

Nevertheless, a decision has to be made soon! I had somewhat realized that Yale wasn't the ultimate situation for me, because Kiphuth didn't have a vision of a full-blown professional preparation program in our field. I felt that there was a possibility of achieving this eventually at The University of Western Ontario. If you want to get to the bottom of my character and personal beliefs, you would know that I'm a great believer in the maximum amount of individual freedom possible for people within the prevailing social environment. Because of that conviction, I've been looking for "the Holy Grail" my whole life. I finally realized that it wasn't ever going to be there at Yale, and that also a person is best advised to make the very best of his or her own present situation—but to keep looking… So I accepted, and we (I, Bert [seven months pregnant!) and young Donald) arrived at Western in August of 1949. I had high hopes of soon guiding the program at Western so well that it would achieve recognized status in a reasonable period of time.

There were many factors leading to their decision to hire me. They knew that I was an assistant line coach at Yale, and they needed a football line coach. They had also wanted to fire this physical education professor who had been picked to head up their embryonic professional program. For some later readily understandable reason, he hadn't seen eye to eye with the athletic director/football coach (John Metras, known as "The Bull"). It turned out, also, that the football coach was on good terms with the president who saw football success as an enhancement to the reputation of the institution. (In retrospect, that should have been a "red light" to me even before I arrived!)

So here I was, up in the purported "land of Indians, Inuits, and skis," to become a department head at the ripe old age of 29. As it then turned out, I served on the job in London, Ontario for about six months and there was "still no action" in the direction of my achieving that administrative status. Eventually, after I expressed some concern, however, the president told me that University was "buying out" the "difficult" department head, as well as threatening to expose some "extra-curricular activity" he was purported to have had. Fortunately, he left quietly, because he was indeed having marital problems. "Higher administration" gave him six months of salary, thereby creating sufficient time for him to complete his dissertation at Columbia. (I don't know that he ever did finish it...) However, I got the position; finally completed my doctorate from Yale; and received the diploma (by mail!) in February of 1951.

(Note: On Saturday, October 1, 1949—we having arrived in London, Ontario in August—our second child, Barbara, was born. The exact timing of her arrival could not be predicted, of course, but everyone of the linemen on our football team knew that I might be "missing a practice" during that week prior to Saturday's home game. One of the linemen had a pool going as to the exact hour "the baby" would arrive! What did happen was that baby Barbara decided her time to come outside of the womb was going to be during the morning of that very Saturday, Oct. 1. However, Barbara dithered, and Bert—after many hours of labor—really did want to "get it done with". So, at 10:00 a.m. that Saturday morning, the birthing physician, who also wanted to get to Saturday afternoon's game, induced labor. Thus, Barbara appeared; he got to the game; and I got to see "Bert and child" before rushing off to coach the line prior to, and during, the game itself. Who did win that game? I think we lost it and several others at the start of that season, but actually Western did win the Canadian title before it was all over that first year.)

My first salary at Western Ontario in 1949 was $4000. It turned out that the only way that I could get the promised total of $4800 as well was to teach two extra courses in German. The president (Dr. Hall) was a bit embarrassed, because he had planned to give me the $4800 from the physical education departmental budget. However I had not quite completed my Ph.D.; so, he also was not yet able to give me the rank of full professor that I achieved subsequently.

> (Note: And, also, he would have been paying me more than the "soon-to-be—gone" department head whom he was trying to "ease out of the door." So I finally had to teach one section of scientific German the first and second term for two years to get the "complete" salary that they had promised me. However, this appointment in the German department for the first two years on campus actually strengthened my status with academic colleagues within the institution.)

When I first went to the University of Western Ontario (now officially called Western University), we were a small department. We had a great relationship with all of the teacher/coaches in the city. I used to meet with them periodically to discuss mutual problems. Also, during one of the last years before I left coaching, I also spoke to 53 elementary schools, PTA's, and similar organizations throughout Ontario as chairman of the Health Education Committee of the Ontario Home and School Association. It actually cost me money to do that; I remember one principal offering me "gum money" collected from disobeying, gum-chewing students! Yet, with all of this "getting around," I got to know the area that Western was supposed to service (i.e., Southwestern Ontario), and in the process also got to know many physical educator/coaches by name. I look back very favorably upon that experience. Further, we also used to bring in London's director of physical education to conduct mock job interviews for senior students in our professional program. Now London is a big city of 400,000 people or more. I don't even know how many high schools there are. There's no longer that "day-to-day relationship" between "town and gown."

## The Idea of a "Unified Program"

Throughout my career at the university level, I've seen the advantages and disadvantages that intercollegiate athletics offers to a departmental program. I was at that point absolutely convinced that physical education and sport could belong together if the situation were such that competitive sport can be kept in sound educational/recreational perspective. If not, forget it! I wanted to see the several programs under one administrative unit that involved the undergraduate, graduate, intramural and intercollegiate programs. That wasn't possible at an Ivy-League institution like Yale where a program in professional preparation for physical education wasn't offered. When I arrived at Western Ontario, the two programs, physical education and athletics, were in the process of splitting up. I presume this was at the instigation of the athletic director (Metras) because he and the department head weren't "seeing eye to eye" on some basic issues. However, I had a joint appointment between physical education and intercollegiate athletics; so, it seemed possible that it could possibly be a happy situation for people thus classified. In addition, based on the president's recommendation, the departmental unit that I headed was to be called it the Department of Physical, Health and Recreation Education. Still further, in addition to the four-year honors B.A. program in physical and health education, we were in the process of starting a second honors B.A. program in recreation education.

One fundamental problem was evident immediately; as department head, I had to go *through* the dean of arts and sciences to bring anything to the president's attention. On the other hand, the athletic director (and head football coach!) had *immediate* access to the president. Because of the influence of football (in Canada too!), he also had access to many of the local alumni, businessmen, and community people who supported the institution. It was an unequal struggle. Yet, there was no way that I was going to knuckle under to unreasonable people or demands. Eventually, after a few years I came into disagreement with the president who didn't share my broader, fuller vision for physical education in a university's overall liberal arts and science program. The dean of what was called "University College" had little respect for my field as well. He was a professor of English who thought that children's "physical education" should be "going out for games" after the regular school day was over… There was no possibility either of developing a master's program as I had hoped would be the case. Although it had intrinsically been a wonderful first experience, I saw that the development at Western wasn't going to materialize in the way that I had hoped *as soon as I had hoped*. Maybe sometime in the future…

## Back to America: "Go Blue"

A colleague, Paul Hunsicker, rescued me from the then deteriorating Western Ontario situation by encouraging the department head, Dr. Elmer D. Mitchell, to hire me at the University of Michigan, Ann Arbor.

*(Note: I've been thinking a lot about Paul recently because the depart- ment at Michigan held a 90th birthday party for Rodney Grambeau, another retired profes- sor there, on Sept. 2, 2010. Of course, Paul himself won't attend, because he is "long gone" having passed away suddenly with a heart attack in 1972 shortly after I had gone back to Western in 1971. Paul really did "save me" in 1956. Yale University had been a good "springboard" in respect to getting another position earlier. However, as far as America was concerned, Western Univer- sity didn't offer much "spring" or "ability to catapult" to a post back in America back then. It was so fortunate for me that I had met Paul at a meeting of the former College Physical Education Association for Men [CPEA] in the early 1950s.*

They say "you make your own luck," and perhaps that's true—but maybe that is so only to a degree. Actually I've been so lucky in a lot of ways. A couple of years after I arrived at Michigan, I was able to advise doctoral studies and pro- mote my areas of scholarly interest within the field. For example, the late Arnold Flath, later head at Oregon State University, was the first doctoral student I advised in the historical aspects of our field. The late Harold VanderZwaag was the first person I advised in the philosophic aspects of the field, and he became well recognized in that area as well as in sport management at the University of Massachusetts subsequently. Then Frank Beeman, now retired from being intra- murals director at Michigan State University, was the first person I advised with a doctoral thesis in sport management theory and practice. I was able to get three different "sub-disciplinary thrusts" going at Michigan in the late 1950s and the early 1960s. This position at Michigan truly got me started in a scholarly way back in the United States again. I began my work there at Michigan in 1956, became chairman of the department of *professional preparation* in physical education in 1961 (not overall physical education!), and left in 1963 when King McCristal offered me the department head position at the University of Illinois (UIUC).

Michigan has a long tradition in physical education, but today the unit is called the School of Kinesiology. That early tradition relates significantly to Elmer Dayton Mitchell, who was still the department head when I first went there. Hunsicker had talked Mitchell into hiring me. However, if Mitchell had really known me, he would *not* have hired me. Mitchell and I were on completely different wavelengths, but Hunsicker assured me: "Don't worry; he's just two years from retirement." Frankly, those were the longest two years of my life! I say this simply because we were indeed "from different worlds" in a variety of ways. I'm not a radical, but I am even at age 93 reasonably far to the left on the educational philosophy spectrum—most any spectrum for that matter—that I later devised and continue to promulgate today. Mitchell was far to the right! Actually, he was at the end of his career; so, certain patterns in practice he had developed (or didn't develop!) within the department were destined to change significantly after he retired.

Nevertheless, Dr. Mitchell came through typically as a nice, well-intentioned man. He goes way back in the early history of the *Research Quarterly* of the American Alliance for Health, Physical Education, Recreation, and Dance. In his personal life he had developed definite interests in bowling in the winter, golf in the summer, and the stock market all year round. He also had his primary responsibility to the department, of course, and a significant responsibility to Prentice-Hall, where he was editor of its physical education series. His priorities were constantly alternating, it seemed. To put it nicely, I felt that the department had been slipping in its standing within the overall field of physical education. Consequently, we all couldn't wait until Dr. Mitchell retired, and then presumably Paul Hunsicker would take over. Another problem at Michigan was that we were in a position of subservience to both intercollegiate athletics and professional education. Michigan, however, was and is a great university (the so-called "Athens of the West"!). Our professional physical education students had an opportunity to relate to the many fine professors within professional education there, as well as in other departments of the University..)

*(Note: Before we leave the "transfer of power" from Mitchell to Hun- sicker, if I may call it that, whenever Dr. Mitchell went out for lunch or coffee "with the boys", he would somehow end up with the check and then laboriously tell each man how much he owed. Somehow his own amount to pay invariably ended up smaller than if the decision had been made by an adding machine. Conversely, Paul Hunsicker, his successor and my "savior," always fought for checks like a tiger, and then had to be forced to divide it up and let others pay their fair share. Interesting example of human nature…)*

Fortunately, Paul Hunsicker, as the new department head, had "navigated" himself and inculcated his ideas generally very nicely. Given his relationship with Willard Olson, the dean in Michigan's School of Education and Fritz Crisler, the director of athletics, it had been apparent that Paul was going to be named the next head of the physical education department. So, just as soon as Mitchell retired, Paul immediately took over. He then had the opportunity to develop the program as he saw fit. He was tremendously interested in physical fitness and chaired the National Physical Fitness Project sponsored by AAHPERD. (This was about the time that President Eisenhower issued "The Report That Shocked the Nation" about overall physical fitness based on some research carried out by Bonnie Pruden, a physiotherapist.) This work by Hunsicker and colleagues encompassed the early youth fitness program along with the development of a manual and tests for national use.

Years later, as Academy president, I had the pleasant experience of presenting the Hetherington Award, the top award of the American Academy of Kinesiology and Physical Education, to Henry Montoye, a leading exercise physiologist and physical educator. While reading the informational statement about him and his background to those in attendance, I mentioned that Dr. Hunsicker had brought Henry Montoye from Michigan State to be on the faculty at the University of Michigan. Subsequently Monty and I sequentially each "jumped ship" as the "first two rats off " at Michigan, Ann Arbor, because at the time—as mentioned earlier—

there were insuperable organization/ structural problems there. Physical education was under *both* education and athletics. The problems seemed insurmountable; so first Monty went to head up the program at Wisconsin, and then a few years later in 2003, I left when the opportunity arose for me to become department head in one of the very top programs in my field at the University of Illinois (UIUC).

## Staley and Illinois Physical Education Development

Before discussing my own experience at Illinois (UIUC) specifically, I think it best to tell something about what had happened earlier at Champaign-Urbana, the twin cities. In the late 1940s, Dean Seward Staley had decided that his unit was going to offer both a master's program and a doctoral program. He asked himself, "Where am I going to find someone who will develop the physical fitness, tests and measurements, physiology, and the kinesiological aspects of our work?" He looked (and asked!) around and finally said, "Tom Cureton's my man." Dr. Cureton accepted the job offer and upon arrival immediately got a strong thrust going in the physical fitness area. His office was always open, and he'd typically say: "Come see me any time." As I learned later, a student would make an appointment and come in with a lot of questions. However, that student typically never got beyond the first question he wanted to ask because Dr. Cureton would lecture on that first question for an hour. By then it was time for the next person!

*(Note: At the symposium held on the occasion of Dr. Staley's much- later 90th birthday, I led off with an historical paper in which I men- tioned that Dr. Cureton's first Ph.D. graduate was Paul Hunsicker. After my talk, I had lunch with Henry Montoye, who had been in the audience. He said with a smile: "By the way, I was the first to finish. My oral exam was in the morning, and Paul's was in the afternoon on the same day." That was the way Cureton did things— busy, busy, busy! A long string of M.A.'s and Ph.D.'s in the physical fitness area followed. Cureton would recruit anyone from any country who ex- pressed even the slightest interest in physical fitness. People used to "accuse him of going down the hall with a vacuum cleaner to pick up these people..." Why? Because he was a true missionary! As Cureton saw it, people who specialized in any area other than physical fitness were obviously following a lesser program and therefore taking a degree of second rank. They were obviously doing this because they simply did not comprehend the importance of physical fitness.)*

## From Ann Arbor, MI to Urbana. IL

Dr. King McCristal, formerly from Michigan State University, was the dean who encouraged me to come to Illinois in 1963. Chet Jackson, the department head, was going to retire at the end of the 1963-64 academic year. Paul Hunsicker, head of the Physical Education Department at Michigan was very gracious about me leaving, even after having just previously given me time off in the middle of the second semester to visit my dying mother, Margery, back in Newport, Vermont. So Bert and I made the decision to hit the road again, and we arrived in Illinois in mid-1963 on a typical, hot, humid day. Then, at the end of the 1963-64 academic year, I became head of the department of physical education for men and head of what arguably was soon the top graduate program in the field.

> *(Note: Incidentally, there's no reason that the head of the men's de- partment should have been head of the joint graduate program any more than the head of the women's department should have been. That was just how it had worked out there as women were gradually achieving more identity and stature in the field. Laura Huelster, the women's head, could have handled such an assignment beautifully, because she was a most capable person).*

My experience at Illinois was tremendous in many ways. A department head had much more power and authority than a department chair. However, I hasten to say that I never even partially used that power in the sense of arbitrarily "ruling the roost." If a majority of the faculty weren't behind any significant move that the department was thinking of making, then it seemed useless to try to move the department in that direction unless I felt I was saving it from extinction or something approximately of that magnitude.

Dean McCristal, a wonderful colleague with whom to work, was also a physical education person who bent over backwards not to show favoritism to the department of physical education for men over other departments and units in the College of Physical Education (i.e., health and safety, recreation and rehabilitation, and intramurals). He was likewise anxious not to show favoritism to the men's department over that of the women. We had joint appointments and so forth; it was very tricky. However, the regular undergraduate program went on separately as normal.

In a relatively short period of time, we developed a very strong social science and humanities thrust to match the quality of the bio-science program effort in our master's and doctoral programs. Among Dr. Cureton, Dr. Hubbard, Dr. Huelster, other fine professors, and myself, we had a quality program rolling. I can take some legitimate credit for that advancement. Before we developed the administrative theory and practice curriculum, for example, there had been only one significant doctoral thesis in America of a truly theoretical nature in that area. We were also able to get a number of people established in sport and physical activity philosophy and in sport and physical education history as well. For example, during my next to the last year at UIUC (before returning to Canada permanently), nine of my doctoral students and five of my master's students finished their theses and dissertations. During the final year, there were 10 more of my doctoral people and three master's people who finished. In retrospect that was far too many to be advising at one time. Nowadays you're hard pressed to find professors, at least at most institutions, who will take on responsibility for several master's or doctoral thesis advisees a given year.

It was interesting—and someone should investigate this from an historical standpoint—that we started pulling in people from all over the British Empire. Starting at the beginning of the 1960s with Nick Strydom from South Africa and John Powell from England, a succession of people from England, Ireland, Wales, Australia and New Zealand, plus a number of top-flight U.S. people, came to Illinois, UIUC to study there. Those people have gone on to perhaps make the most significant contribution to this field in second half of the 20th century at the university level, other than perhaps the earlier contribution made by Columbia Teachers College and New York University earlier when graduate programs were introduced. I could take you into the roster of the American Academy of Kinesiology and Physical Education (now the NAK) and point out all of these people that are in the Academy as a result of that Illinois development and its aftermath. A number of them went back to their own countries, of course, but the enormous "brain drain" from Loughborough University in England alone who functioned all over the place: Mike Wade at Minnesota; Mike Ellis at Illinois, Karl Newell at Penn State, Glyn Roberts, at Illinois and a "seemingly endless group" of people from elsewhere (e.g., Dan Landers and Bob Osterhoudt from Arizona State).

## PART III

# "The Illinois Slush-Fund Scandal"

The following is my version of what happened to intercollegiate athletics in a great educational institution in the late 1960s. It is called "The Illinois Slush- Fund Scandal of the 1960s". The various topics included will be discussed in the following order: (a) Announcement of the "Irregularities"; (b) The Big Ten Investigation & Search for a New Athletic Director; (c) The University's Appeal & The Subsequent Decision; (d) The Search for New Coaches; (e) Results of NCAA Deliberations; and (f) Conclusions and Discussion.

## Announcement of the "Irregularities

In November of 1966, Doug Mills, who had been Director of Intercollegiate Athletics at the University of Illinois for twenty-five years, decided to retire. After he resigned from his post, a search for his successor began. Pete Elliott, the Head Football Coach at Illinois, was mentioned prominently among the candidates for the position.

On December 17, 1966, it was reported that Big Ten Commissioner Bill Reed had issued the following statement on December 16 concerning Illinois' recruiting practices:

> Dr. David D. Henry, President of the University of Illinois, has reported to me Friday that there have been brought to his attention certain irregularities with respect to grants-in-aid assistance to athletes at the university.

He believes that he is in possession of all the facts and has invited my inquiry into the matter with the offer of full cooperation on the part of the university in any investigation I may wish to undertake.

I will begin the investigation in accordance with regular conference procedures and will have no further comment until it is completed (The News-Gazette, Dec. 17, 1966).

To those close to the scene, it quickly became apparent what had brought on this unusual situation. Mel Brewer, the Assistant Athletic Director, learned that Pete Elliott, the Head Football Coach, was about to be named as the person to succeed Doug Mills, the retiring Athletic Director. Thinking about his many years of loyal service to Illinois, Brewer became extremely upset that he was not being recommended for the post. He decided to reveal to President Henry a number of infractions of the rules that had occurred, infractions in which Elliott, Harry Combes (Basketball Coach), and Howie Braun (Assistant Basketball Coach) had been involved. These rule violations in regard to financial aid presumably implicated a total of twelve tendered athletes in football and basketball (*The Daily Illini*, Dec. 17, 1964.)

The immediate aftermath of the announcement was predictable. The story became a "media bonanza" all over the country. In 1967 this story, and what subsequently transpired, was selected in the twin cities of Champaign-Urbana where the University is located, as the leading, local-event news story of the year (*The Urbana Courier*, Dec. 31, 1967). Mel Brewer offered his resignation from Intercollegiate Athletics shortly after the disclosure, even though he retained a twenty-five percent teaching responsibility with the Department of Physical Education for Men, an assignment that had been handled capably over the years. His resignation from Athletics was accepted as of January 31, 1967. Mr. Brewer was criticized in many quarters as a "Judas" because of the timing of his release of the information. Loren Tate, a local sports columnist, wrote:

Mel Brewer, the man who drilled the holes in the side of the ship, is no longer welcome, however. His revelations have shocked a university president whose ears never should have been dented with this sort of thing. In his world, President Henry cannot be expected to comprehend the jungle that is Big Ten athletics (The News-Gazette, Dec. 21, 1966).

> *(Note: It is somewhat difficult to accept such pontification on the part of Mr. Tate who was fully aware of the fact that Intercollegiate Athletics at Illinois was under the direct supervision of the President's Office. However, it must be appreciated that this affair became a sensation and a newspaper "soap opera" overnight with most of the members of the local and "alumni" community eagerly awaiting the following day's installment. For example, three star basketball players had been declared ineligible at that time, also. Thus, with the entire community caught up in the developing true-life drama, the sports editors were literally in their glory as both narrators and oracles.) (2)*

## The Big Ten Investigation: Search for a New Athletic Director

On Friday, December 22, 1966 (only three days before Christmas Day!), the Big Ten and NCAA officials met for eleven hours in a closed session. Illinois officials, Vice-President Herbert Farber and Acting Athletic Director Les Bryan, submitted the actual documents that had been received by President Henry from Mr. Brewer. The next steps were for Bill Reed, the Big Ten Commissioner, to present the facts to the nine Athletic Directors for a ruling, and also for Arthur Bergstrom, Assistant Executive Director of the National Collegiate Athletic Association, to forward the evidence of the infractions to the appropriate committee for a ruling at the national level (*The Courier*, December 23, 1966).

It soon became evident that various people and representatives of the press were looking for scapegoats. For example, Bill Reed was being criticized for the suspension of the three basketball players in mid-season, but it turned out that officials at Illinois had initiated a request for such a status themselves (*The Courier*, December 24, 1966). Further, Reed indicated that the University had indeed turned over a set of meticulous records indicating that a total of twenty-nine athletes had received emergency-need and/or travel payments. He stressed further that "everything" had been in the hands of a local businessman, and that donations to the fund had been solicited from friends and alumni of the University. The sums of money granted were actually very small, relatively speaking, a fact that caused the Commissioner to remark: "I don't know why it was felt necessary to give excessive aid when legitimate loan funds are available on the campus" (*Ibid.*).

By the first of the New Year (1967), it became apparent that this affair was going to have to grind itself out, and also that a new athletic director had to be chosen. Daily articles and opinion columns appeared in the three local newspapers, coverage that was embellished by comments from other sections of the state, region, and nation. The system was blamed; the alumni were blamed; local businessmen were blamed; the administrators were blamed; the coaches were blamed; and the athletes were blamed. A persistent theme that emerged was "others are doing it; why can't we?" An editorial in *The Daily Illini* complained that: "The United States is the only nation in the world which tries to uphold this idealistic attitude toward amateur athletics. If our rules governing amateurs were in line with those of other nations, we would walk away with almost every gold medal at the Olympics ... (January 5, 1967).

In an interesting issue of *The Daily Illini*, dated Jan. 14, 1967, the headline stated "Big Questions Still Unanswered," and then Dan Balz, the Sports Editor, delineated what he called "new facts and statements." For example, he stated that Mel Brewer had had no direct contact with President Henry-that he had simply reported the fact to Les Bryan, the Acting Athletic Director , on December 7. Further, he stated that there were three, not two, illegal funds as had been reported earlier. The "books" on these funds had presumably been kept by Bill Burrows, an employee of Bailey and Himes, a local sporting goods company, and also presumably "on the request of Doug Mills, former athletic director." Still further, Balz reported that "many of the payments made to the athletes would have been approved, had they gone through legitimate channels." Finally, Balz stated that it was known that "the athletes received no hearing before they were suspended" (*The Daily Illini*, Jan. 14, 1967, p. 1).

In the meantime, a number of different names were being mentioned as possibilities for the vacant post of athletic director. However, Gene Vance, the 43-year old Alumni Director of the University, was named as the fourth athletic director in the University's history. Vance was indeed a member of the "Illinois family". He had played guard on two championship basketball teams in 1942 and 1943 with Doug Mills as his head coach. Now, while waiting until April 1 when he was scheduled to assume the position, he stated: "I plan to spend time with Dr. Bryan to get background on the situation and talk to the coaches and their staffs" (*The News-Gazette*, January 17, 1967).

For the next five to six weeks, the local and regional newspapers were full of reports, statements, counter-statements, rumors, letters to the editor, and similar items. In his annual State of the University Report under II (Some Current Issues), President Henry wrote "I am deeply disappointed that representatives of the Athletic Association have been responsible for infractions of the regulations of the Intercollegiate (Big Ten) Conference . . . No university can tolerate a double standard in keeping its agreements" (*The Urbana Courier*, Jan. 21, 1967). Exactly one month later (February 22, 1967), President Henry learned that the Big Ten Athletic Directors agreed with him strongly. The directors voted to force Illinois to dismiss the three coaches involved (Elliott, Combes, and Braun).

President Henry, after discussing the matter with the University's legal counsel, James J. Costello, immediately announced his intention to appeal what he considered to be a "too harsh" penalty. Such an appeal had to be made to the final arbiters, the faculty representatives of the Big Ten. It was this group that also had the responsibility of deciding what would happen to the twelve athletes who had been declared ineligible by the University itself when the violations had been disclosed (*The Urbana Courier*, February 23, 1967).

### The University's Appeal: The Subsequent Decision

Even though there was no reason to think that any ruling would be a light one, so to speak, and even though the "show cause" rule (as it was called) indicated that a university's membership in the conference could be terminated or suspended for infractions, most university officials and others involved in some way with Illinois felt the ruling was too harsh, was unfair, and represented a "crushing blow" to the University's athletic future (*The News-Gazette*, Feb. 23, 1967). However, an editorial in *The Daily Illini* ended with the following words: "It often is harder to acknowledge that a good friend has done something wrong. But when the evidence is there, there is little room for discussion. We agree with the Big Ten" (February 24, 1967). Another column written by Bob Strohm was entitled "Misplaced Loyalty." It refers to "Captain Henry." and stated the following: "As for the childish rationalizations conjured up by almost everyone under the spell of 'spunky' Dr. Henry (that) 'Everyone else is doing it; why should we get punished?' That brand of thought is most often heard by grade school teachers" (*Ibid.*).

Based on the ensuing publicity—although others expressing similar opinions most often declined to be named (!)—it was obvious that *The Daily Illini* and a few others were in the minority. Two different petitions urging that the coaches be retained were circulated by some alumni and some football players. The President of the Illinois High School Coaches' Association moved to get the state's coaches behind the University's appeal (*The News Gazette*, February 25, 1967). All eighty-two members of the football squad signed a petition. The Board of Directors of the Athletic Association met to affirm its support of the coaches. Hal McCoy in *The Detroit Free Press* stated: "It's not Illinois on trial. It's the Big Ten..." (February 25, 1967). In the Illinois State Legislature, the House debated a resolution asking for leniency, but finally decided that the legislature shouldn't get involved at that point *(The News-Gazette*, March 2, 1967). Even the Honorable Otto Kerner, Governor of Illinois, took up the cause for Illinois. "I know Pete Elliott particularly. There's no finer, cleaner man. If my son were at the University and were working under Pete Elliott, I would be delighted. He's the type of man I'd like my son to associate with" (*The Urbana Courier*, February 27, 1967). (*Interestingly, but sadly, the Governor himself went to jail as the result of a racetrack scandal and pay-off a bit later.*)

All of the pleas were in vain, however, because on March 3, 1967, the faculty representatives of the Big Ten Conference sent a telegram to President Henry stating that the Commissioner be notified by March 17 whether the three coaches would be retained. "If the answer is 'no' the case is closed. If the answer to the question is 'yes' as to any of these coaches, will you then discuss with the commissioner dates convenient for a hearing at which the university is invited to show cause why its membership in the conference should not be suspended or terminated?" (*The Urbana Courier*, March 4, 1967. On the next day, two basketball players, Rich Jones and Ron Dunlop were declared permanently ineligible, as was football halfback, Cyril Pinder, along with four unnamed athletes (*The News-Gazette*, March 5, 1967).

It wasn't all over yet. On Monday, March 7, Henry issued a statement that he intended to carry the matter through with a final appeal on the March 17 deadline that he had been given. Governor Kerner expressed his support for Illinois again, and the entire Board of Trustees backed the President's stance as well. Then, if matters weren't bad enough, Irv Kupcinet, a Chicago columnist, reported that Doug Mills, the retired athletic director, told him that Henry "knew as much about the fund as I did" (*The Sun-Times*, March 12, 1967) Mills denied this immediately saying that Kupcinet had somehow misinterpreted him. "Nothing could be farther from the truth. There is no more honest man than Dr. Henry (*The News-Gazette*, March 13, 1967). No matter who was right, who was wrong, who

was misinterpreted, and who wasn't, the absolutely final appeal was unequivocally denied by the Big Ten Conference. "If after March 21 (Tuesday), coaches Elliott, Combes, and Braun, or any one of them, be retained ... the membership of the University of Illinois ... shall be suspended as of that date ... (*The News-Gazette*, March 19, 1967).

Thus, what had seemed almost inevitable occurred on March 21—the three coaches filed their resignations. Their statement expressed deep appreciation for the support that they had received from President Henry and "alumni, students, faculty, and friends" of the University, but no mention was made of the violations of the rules by any of them. They hoped that their resignations would result in the "amelioration of the penalties imposed on the students..." (*The Urbana Courier*, March 20, 1967).

## The Search for New Coaches

Although some may disagree, it could be argued that what happened after this is almost completely anticlimactic in nature. Tate stated that "the coaches took the honorable route" (*The News-Gazette*, March 20, 1967), whereas on the same day Bertine made the same assessment and wrote a second column in which he discussed "the many questions left in the wake of the coaches' resignations" (*The Urbana Courier*, March 20, 1967). It was explained that the search for new coaches had already begun, and that "this job will become the first major responsibility of Gene Vance when he assumes the athletic directorship on April l" (*The News-Gazette*, March 20, 1967). Even the histories of the three coaches were traced at length in *The Urbana Courier* (March 20, 1967). (Since all of these were separate articles, one wonders what space was left for any other news in the newspapers on this day.)

On the next day (March 21, 1967), The Daily Illini told about a highly condemnatory editorial in *The Chicago Tribune* criticizing the Big Ten itself for its hypocritical action "when all the men have academic standing in the School of Physical Education." (One interesting sidelight at that time was that a mammoth testimonial dinner was held in Champaign-Urbana for the three coaches and their wives at which an unnamed co-chairman stated that "Our goal is to raise #10,000 cash for each of the three coaches. We can't do enough for these men," *The Chicago Tribune*, March 23, 1967. Each of the wives received a star-sapphire wristwatch at this dinner, and there was also discussion of starting a fund to have statues of the three coaches erected in a prominent location!) Such a plan never materialized to the best of my knowledge.

Shortly thereafter, the new head coaches for football and basketball were announced. They were James Valek, who was immediately released from his position there by South Carolina, and Harve Schmidt, who was also immediately released from the University of New Mexico. Loren Tate, in *The News-Gazette* stated boldly "Two former University of Illinois athletics greats have been designated to lead the Fighting Illini out of the 'slush fund' quagmire" (March 29, 1967). Illinois had decided to stay within its own "athletic family."

## Results of NCAA Deliberations

It was not until May 7, 1967 that the National Collegiate Athletic Association announced its decision about possible penalties to be imposed upon the University of Illinois. As might have been expected, the NCAA decided that Illinois would be barred from Rose Bowl consideration for two years, and further that there would be no post-season competition in basketball. The biggest concern in athletic circles in the Champaign-Urbana area seemed to be that this might be disappointing to the athletes and thereby cut down on their incentive to win. Further, it was felt that recruiting for the next few years would be hampered as well (*The Urbana Courier*, May 8, 1967). On top of this, just eleven days later, the faculty representatives of the Big Ten Conference denied a petition asking for modification of the ineligibility penalties against certain of the athletes involved (*The News-Gazette*, May 19, 1967). Then, on April 24, a committee of the Illinois State Legislature brought forward a 180-page draft report recommending that Big Ten and NCAA investigations should be independent of one another "as this is not a country designed as were the occupied countries of the collaborationist Hitler regime" (*The News-Gazette*, May 24, 1967). (It will be left to the reader's imagination to decipher that enigmatic statement.)

## Discussion

A narrative such as this must be concluded at some point, although it should be stated again that many ramifications of this unpleasant situation simply could not be included in what must be considered to be a preliminary analysis. Nevertheless, a study of this type should necessarily arrive at some conclusions and offer further discussion. Although further study may either substantiate or correct what will now be said, the following thoughts seem to be reasonable ones at this point:

> Preservation of what has been termed "the amateur ideal" has always been a problem in U.S. competitive sport at the intercollegiate level (Flath, 1964). The excesses of the early twentieth century, for example, have been amply described in the now famous Carnegie Foundation report (*American College Athletics*) that stressed that the prevailing amateur code had been violated continually (1929). In colleges and universities where gate receipts were important, these excesses have continued on unabated despite the well-meaning intentions of many who were concerned. There have been periodic investigations, books written, and commissions established, all resulting in hand-wringing and subsequent condemnation. However, these responses to the flagrant excesses have generally been to no avail.

Although it is true that these evils have been exposed actually in only a relatively few colleges and universities, intercollegiate athletics has resultantly been marred because of an enormous quantity of highly unfavorable media attention. (Maybe this is so because people have a right to expect something more wholesome from institutions of higher education.) However, what has happened, and what has been reported, have strongly influenced the "atmosphere and mentality" of college and high school athletics generally. Moreover, somehow highly competitive sport in the United States has taken on a life of its own above (or below!) the espoused values and norms of the society

Preservation of "the amateur ideal" has always been a problem in U.S. competitive sport at the intercollegiate level (Flath, 1964). The excesses of the early twentieth century, for example, have been amply described in the now famous Carnegie Foundation report (*American College Athletics*) that stressed the continual violation of the amateur code (1929). In colleges and universities where gate receipts were important, these excesses have continued on unabated despite the well-meaning intentions of concerned citizens. There have been periodic investigations, books written, and commissions established, all resulting in hand-wringing and subsequent condemnation. However, responses to the flagrant excesses have generally been to no avail.

## Specific Conclusions

1. Breaking the rules has a "long history" in U. S. intercollegiate athletics.

2. The social forces at work (e.g., the society's values and norms) are evidently not sufficiently strong to permanently rectify the illegal and dishonorable situation that prevails in the gate-receipt sports throughout the land (see discussion below).

3. Inasmuch as the amateur/professional controversy has consistently been marred by illogicality and inconsistency, the possibility and practicality of "legal semi-professionalism" should be considered as one way out of this ongoing serious societal problem.

4. Humans under pressure reveal frailties in all types of situations, including those that arise in intercollegiate athletics. The people involved at Illinois are seemingly no better and no worse than others involved in such practices

in the past and at present. Although the three coaches and others "sinned, these transgressions were venial, not mortal, in nature. "

5.  It will undoubtedly take unusual, outstanding individual and collective leadership to resolve the longstanding, shameful situation in intercollegiate athletics that makes a mockery of espoused national ideals, not to mention what it does to the "soul" of those colleges and universities that are involved.

## Concluding Statement

Finally, it can be stated that we simply do not seem to learn from past mistakes. For example, in 1981 Illinois was again placed on a three years' probation by unanimous vote of the Big Ten Conference's faculty representatives. Further, even as this paper was being prepared, fresh, new penalties are to be imposed on Illinois in 1984-85. One can only speculate as to whether such travesties exhibited in the name of higher education will ever end. It is important to say that this historical summary and analysis relates the trials and tribulations of one university only in the sphere of intercollegiate athletics. Obviously, there have been and are many others caught in the throes of so-called amateur sport that—when you get right down to it—is really semi-professional. However, it must be said also that what has been stated here cannot be regarded as representative of what goes on in competitive sport in the majority of colleges and universities in North America (i.e., the outright cheating and defiance). For them intercollegiate sport is still a socially useful servant in the education of both young men and (now) young women. For their sake—for our culture's sake!—this type of smear or blot on sport's escutcheon cannot be tolerated indefinitely. In the United States especially, "present-day slaves doing combat in the arena deserve a far better fate in the land of the free and home of the brave." To conclude, "if men could learn from history, what lessons it might teach us" (Coleridge).

## Reference Notes

1.  Any historical study has limitations. In this study it must be explained that the investigator was the head of the Department of Physical Education for Men (and Graduate Chairman) at the University of Illinois, Champaign-

Urbana, from 1964-1968. There are points within this narrative where some personal reference might have been made to a letter written to a dean, a comment made in response to a reporter's question, what would have been said at a committee meeting held by the Illinois State Legislature if such a statement had been permitted, what was told to him "off the record," etc., but these were insignificant and tangential only in the drama that was unfolding. Every effort has been made to keep personal bias from this paper. Further, appreciation should be expressed to Dr. Melvin Adelman, The Ohio State University, for his assistance in the collating of data during the time when these incidents were taking place. However, he is not responsible for any opinions, errors or omissions in this narrative.

2.  *It is interesting to note here that people on campus in administrative posts were in no way kept informed on the developments taking place. This is the main reason why this investigator kept such a careful record through the three newspapers of what was transpiring. **It is also interesting to conjecture why the reporters were kept so well informed, while campus administrators with a legitimate claim to knowledge were told absolutely nothing.** Even though the three coaches, and sixteen others, were on his departmental budget anywhere from ten to seventy-five percent (and a number of these men held university tenure), this investigator had no way of knowing what was occurring and to what extent the Department's reputation might become tarnished in the process. Despite a series of letters and memoranda sent to others who might enlighten departmental personnel, no satisfactory responses were received. (A copy of a detailed letter sent on February 27, 1967 asking for tangible information is available from the investigator upon request.)*

## References

Carnegie Foundation for the Advancement of Teaching, The. *American College Athletics*. (H. J. Savage et al., eds.). New York: The Foundation, Bulletin #23, 1929.

*Chicago Tribune, The*, March 23, 1967.

*Courier, The* (Urbana), Dec. 23, 1966, Dec. 24, 1966, Jan. 21, 1967, Feb. 27, 1967, March 4, 1967, March 20, 1967, May 8, 1967, Dec. 31, 1967.

*Daily Illini, The.* Dec. 17, 1966, Jan. 5, 1967, Jan. 14, 1967, Feb. 24, 1967, March 21, 1967.

*Detroit Free Press, The,* Feb. 25, 1967.

Flath, A. W. *A history of the relations between the National Collegiate Athletic Association and the Amateur Athletic Union of the United States (1905-1963).* Champaign, IL: Stipes Publishing Co., 1964.

*News-Gazette, The,* Dec. 17, 1966, Dec. 21, 1966, Jan. 10, 1967, Jan. 17, 1967, Feb. 23, 1967, Feb. 25, 1967, March 2, 1967, March 5, 1967, March 13, 1967, March 19, 1967, March 20, 1967, March 22, 1967, March 29, 1967, May 24, 1967

# Life After the Illinois "Debacle"

Unfortunately, the "climate" in the professional physical education area was "sharply disturbed" when The "Illinois Slush Fund Scandal" broke in 1967. There were 17 coaches on my departmental payroll anywhere from 10 percent to 75 percent in the physical education unit. In total, there were 130 people on the payroll, including instructors and graduate assistants. These figures were for just the men's department; obviously, it was a very large program. As this scandal developed, it turned out that the head and assistant basketball coaches, *and* the head football coach, were caught up in the situation. And I, as department head could not find out *anything* about the status of these three people who had appointments in my department! "Everything" went completely into the Office of the President that "took it over", so to speak.

So I said to Dean McCristal, "We've got to get to the bottom of this. Are we going to break tenure on these people if they're proven guilty?" I can remember King saying: "Don't worry; I'll make an appointment with President Henry." A few days later, on the way over to a meeting he scheduled, King said, "Now, don't disagree with him about *anything*." I turned around and started walking the other way just for the hell of it. He said, "Where are you going, where are you going?" I said, "There's no point in going to have an interview if I can't ask questions and respond to what I might disagree with." He said, "Well, just be very gentle about it because university presidents get "caught up" in this business. They *have to* support the athletics enterprise. If they don't, they'll lose their jobs." This was the sad fact about Division I and Division II athletics functioning within the National

College Athletic Association in America. *(As is well known, this fact is well known down to the present. The situation today is, of course, even worse!*

I soon found that—physically, emotionally, what have you?, I simply couldn't physically bear any more of such shenanigans at this Illinois scene. Yet I hated to give up my position as department head of one of the top such programs in America! Somehow, however, the whole situation just "got to me," and the next thing I knew I had a duodenal spasm. I didn't even know what *that* was! I'd never had anything like of that nature in my life, although I knew my father had a "sensitive" stomach. Hence, I discovered that I too must have a fairly sensitive one… I said to my doctor: "What *is* this?" He said, "In a university town we call it department heads' malady." I said, "No, joking aside, what is it technically?" He replied: "It's a duodenal spasm." When I asked what that was, he said, "Well, if you get several of them, you will probably get an ulcer." I shuddered; went home;  and said to my wife: "Life's too short for this nonsense".

> *(Note: When I first met my father and my one half brother, I was 28 years of age. They both looked at me and said, "Have you ever had an ulcer?" I said, "No." They said, "Well, we have." Then they looked at my legs and said, "We both have bowed legs and yours are straight." I said: "Guess that came from my mother.")*

So I immediately wrote a letter to Dean McCristal saying (1) that **if *we* weren't going to be involved in the resolution of these problems of our own faculty members**, and (2) **the University couldn't keep athletics under control**—I reluctantly **"wanted out of the administrative part of my position"** such as it had proved to be.

Thinking back, at both Yale and Western Ontario (the first time I worked at "Western:"), and then when I worked at Michigan from 1956 to 1963, I had believed that athletics were basically on "the up and up"… Oh, I had heard about an alumnus "slipping something to this or that athlete here and there". When I had started to work at Michigan, for example, we used to go to all of the home football games mostly to watch the band! The football team was losing (i.e., in retrospect, does that mean they were honest?). In my opinion Michigan had, and still has, the best band with which to "serenade" its typical 115,000 spectators! Illinois had only *once* been winners in football or basketball. That was in 1963, the year I arrived, when Illinois actually went to the Rose Bowl.

However, they had evidently been cheating in regard to illegal financial aid for athletes before and after the date that the so-called "Slush-Fund Scandal" broke— and at that point I learned additionally that they'd been caught several times. (It is my understanding that the situation at Illinois has been turned around considerably by sound leadership since.) So what happens in physical education departments at such institutions? (I'm thinking of my associates at Pennsylvania State University as I write these words—obvious a different sort of a situation, however.) People typically say, "Oh, we don't have any trouble with athletics; they're over there." However, as far as I was concerned, we in physical (activity) education *are* athletics or sport too—**and they are "us"!** Physical activity education and sport should be "one family". By that I mean that we are both concerned with the place of developmental physical activity in the lives of people. We should be employing such "movement"—such developmental physical activity—to help people "live life healthily and fully." However, the extent to which athletics has become commercialized and sensationalized simply means that purposes other than the primacy of the individual's all-round development are being served.

The men's and women's departments combined a bit later after I left the University of Illinois? It was evidently a "shotgun marriage" by administrative fiat. And no one could foresee that at the end of the 1960s there would be a tremendous glut of people wanting positions working in higher education. All of a sudden, the roof started falling in financially. Nevertheless, it seemed as though wherever one turned there were funding cutbacks. This happened at Illinois as well.

## "Canada, Here We Come Back Again"!

I continued as a professor in the department for the next two years, but the die had been cast! Illinois had one of the several top graduate programs at the time; *so, there was nowhere else for me to go in my field!* For example, the "Ivy League" didn't sponsor graduate programs. Also, it was difficult staying there at Illinois because the new department head seemed to feel "uneasy" about my ongoing presence. Perhaps it was "unconscious" on his part, but he seemed to want to "put me in my 'new place' even though I had hired him!"

So without hesitation I decided to come back to Canada in 1971 when a position as dean became available in what was planned as a new faculty (i.e., college/ school). I did so even though technically I didn't leave employment at Illinois until 1972. It was agreed that I should take a leave of absence from Illinois during the 1971—72 academic year. This was arranged so that they wouldn't lose the budget line because of developing financial strictures of the period.

> *(Note: That arrangement turned out to be a great help to me finan- cially as well, because my pension evidently became "vested" with that one more year of credit [to which the University and I both contributed]. As I am writing these words, I have been receiving a partial, monthly pension from the State of Illinois for 27 years! In addition, even though I knew I wasn't going back, that so-called leave of absence was further a safety valve in case I got to The University of Western Ontario and found that I'd made an awful mistake by returning there. As it turned out, although a variety of problems did develop after a few years, the move back was essentially "a god one"!)*

Interestingly, I never thought I'd go back to Canada and especially not to Western University (as it now called)! Yet, when the time came that it seemed best to do so—that's the only way it could be worked out. I confess that my disenchantment with America had been growing slowly but steadily anyhow. Why so? Because I simply could not see any hope of the situation in intercollegiate athletics changing for the better anywhere that I might conceivably be employed. (As I mentioned above, the fine "Ivy-League" institutions did not "deign" to offer professional study in my field.) Everything considered, therefore, it worked out extremely well for me at that point. In addition, my good friend and colleague, Garth Paton, was on the search committee for the new faculty at Western as well. He had earlier joined me as a graduate student as Michigan to do his M.A. degree, and then subsequently completed his doctoral dissertation with my supervision at Illinois. Fortunately, there was also a fine academic vice-president (Dr.

Roger Rossiter) at Western Ontario at this point, and I just knew he'd be a good person with whom to work.

Once again I found myself thinking: "Gee, this is finally it!" When they offered me the job, it was odd how some surprising things happened shortly after that. In the fall of 1971, just after I accepted the job as dean of the new Faculty of Physical Education at Western, I received a rather desperate call from the University of Oregon. My friend, Jan Broekhoff, said, "Please come out right away! The job is just about yours if you want it!" Hence, although I had just accepted the position at Western Ontario, I have thought of Oregon several times since because of my favorable earlier relationship with Art Esslinger, Harrison Clarke, and others fine professors there. Nevertheless, lurking in the back of my mind was the thought that—once again (!) if I accepted an American position—I'd be in one of those "untenable" university positions where intercollegiate football—and all that this entails!—somehow "rules the roost"!

> *Note: I should explain what eventually did happen at he University of Oregon. Actually Jan Broekhoff himself accepted was finally offered the dean's post and then, subsequently, because of financial reasons, Oregon phased out the College! I recall attending a "wake" about the College's demise at an AAHPERD convention session that Jan himself chaired (while he was actually dying of cancer, also). It was so very sad...*

Soon after my arrival back at Western in 1971, I had an interview with the President Williams and Vice President Rossiter. I said to these men, "Just give' us a "fair shake" in this new faculty. We also have 42 sports within intercollegiate athletics: 21 for men and 21 for women. I want to have an outstanding intramural program too. We can continue nicely the present development in that program, because students pay a regular fee that we can adjust annually to the cost of living. We have a fine undergraduate program with hundreds of students, also, and a graduate program that I'd like to expand beyond the master's degree to the doctoral level. For example, I'd like to initiate a program with *both* a bioscience component and a social science and humanities component too. We could soon have one of the best programs in the world." They said, "Fine, what do you need to get started?" I said, "$300,000." They said, "Okay, to meet this request we'll give you an additional $100,000 for each of the next three years." As it turned out, we got the first $100,000, but we never saw the other $200,000! In Ontario the "financial roof for education had fallen in once again".

Interestingly, I hadn't known that the two men with whom I discussed the future of our faculty (i.e., the president and the vice-president) also happened to have become mortal enemies. Not too many people knew why Dr. Roger Rossiter, a fine man and a biochemist from "down under", soon after resigned his post as vice president of academics to become vice president of health sciences. President Carlton Williams then brought in Grant Reuber, the dean of social science, as the new vice president of academics. Dr. Williams, a nice man, was not a president who would be sincerely involved with the concerns of our new faculty. I soon learned this fact at a budget meeting with Reuber and Al Adlington, the vice president of finance. "Herr" Reuber immediately gave me the impression that he was trying forthrightly to match that famous Nazi of World War II notoriety. Dr. Rossiter, my first superior when I returned, had been interested in all aspects of the program at Western. And our department had been given permission by the Province of Ontario to go ahead with a proposed doctoral program, because Western had earlier established the first master's program in our field.

Nonetheless, Reuber and the graduate dean (Stewart) soon showed "significant disinterest" in that direction. Also, Reuber didn't want *anything* to do with intramurals or intercollegiate athletics. He said, "In terms of the budget, those two programs belong with non-academic items." It soon became apparent that he wasn't going to give our academic program any special favors either. So, we obviously were facing a difficult struggle, and we just had to make our way as best possible...

*Note: Years later, after I had bowed out of administration at Western because of the lack of respect and concern for our field shown by this vice-president academic (Reuber) and Dean Stewart, our faculty finally did receive approval for a doctoral program in the bioscience aspects of our field. I should explain that the graduate dean was a biochemist. However, he simply couldn't visualize such an entity as a social science and humanities component to physical education and sport. (Recall that developing that latter was one of the reasons I had gone back there!)*

Other than this basic struggle with "higher administration", however, things got rolling quite nicely. Yet money had again become tight at Western. Moreover, there just was no way that I was going to be a "yes man" for that "replacement" vice president of academics. This "character" literally said to me at one point: "Zeigler, You are playing on the wrong ball team." (I guess he thought that I could understand "sportspeak" better…) I saw myself as representative of my faculty, of course, the person who would promote and help my faculty members realize their personal ambitions within the scope of the faculty's purpose and aims. He saw me more as the person who kept the faculty "sullen but not mutinous" while he, the all- wise vice-president academic, decided which programs would be the beneficiaries of his "royal favor" in respect to a greater monetary allotment…

Later we had one *unique* budgetary session when times were tough ("When weren't they"?), and "Herr" Reuber handed the actual intramural athletics budget and intercollegiate athletics budget pages to the vice president of administration & finance and said: "Here, Al, you take this." Adlington replied: "I don't want them; they belong to you." They continued to swear back and forth jocularly at each other; so finally I said in the prevailing vernacular, "Will you guys make up your minds as to where the hell you think we belong, because theoretically I believe that at Western it had been decided that we belonged together under one administrative unit". While this dialogue was taking place, this "nice" president (Carlton Williams) was sitting casual and relaxed at the head of the table looking at some papers.

It was obvious that he really just didn't want to be bothered with this boring budgetary hearing anyhow. Evidently he had arranged for his secretary to come in after he had been in this meeting for about 10 minutes and say, "Dr. Williams, there's an important long distance call for you." So he gathered up his papers, left, and I faced the struggle alone with these two "clowns". (In addition, J. P. Metras, the former football coach and athletic director, was still kicking around on campus, and he had continued as "good friends" and "drinking buddies" with that "other" vice president! This probably resulted in "inside information" about our faculty [and *his* former intercollegiate athletics program!] being passed along for Adlington to add to his "fount of knowledge"…)

So, everything considered, in the fourth year of my appointment I started to realize sadly that I wasn't doing my administrative unit much good at this point constantly having to "battle" with these men. Certainly I wasn't going to make much headway in the near future either. I was struggling; my faculty colleagues were powerless; and our faculty unit as a whole was making slow progress. Hence, in the final analysis it seemed to me that the Faculty and I would each do better if I became just a *full* professor.

> *(Note: Originally, when I had asked how long the term as dean was, they told me that it was either five or seven years. They said, "We hope it's seven." I said jokingly: "You may want to get rid of me at the end of the fifth year; so let's leave it flexible".)*

So, I went to President Williams and said, "Why don't I ask you to invoke that option for a five-year term?" Hence I was released at the end of five years. I confess that I wasn't too thrilled about leaving my administrative post, because I had a lot of life in me yet, and I had indeed moved the program forward. However, I had wanted to move it even further! With me phasing out, Vice President Reuber, "in his wisdom," saw to it that the dean's position was filled by the former *department* head, the man who had also succeeded me as head so long ago when I left to

go to Michigan in 1956. This man then became more or less of a "caretaker dean," having been selected when the leading candidate for the post—an outside candidate—dropped dead! (I couldn't believe it!) This was just fine for VP (Herr!) Reuber, because he didn't see our field moving ahead very much any way, certainly not the way I had wanted to see it move.

## A Mere Full Professor Once Again...

So, there I was after five extremely busy, essentially rewarding years as the dean of a new faculty at The University of Western Ontario—the place where I had first become an administrator "in another country at another time" (i.e., 1950). Once again I was *just* a professor! In retrospect I was so fortunate that, as a dean involved heavily in administration, I had not abandoned typical professional duties including teaching, scholarship and professional involvements as the large majority of people do who take on such managerial posts. Somehow, by working sufficient hours for a job and a half (i.e., about 65 or more hrs. weekly), I had managed to continue with a full teaching load during my years as dean. Then, too, I had not slackened with my "writing", publications, and outside professional "responsibilities." Hence I was in a position to continue as a full professor at the peak of my career. During the years from 1978 to 1984—and from then to 1989, semi-retired, but teaching part time—I continued "full steam ahead" with teaching, writing, research, professional contributions, and presentations all over North America and in many foreign countries as well.

It had been my practice since my stay at Michigan, Ann Arbor—mainly because of annual faculty reviews for possible promotion and salary increases— to list all such activities needed to construct such a "progress report" month by month, year by year from the beginning of my career down to the present. When I was at Yale in the 1940s, there really wasn't anything "professional" to report; it wasn't that type of a post where promotions were possible. Physical education was just a service program for freshmen and a recreational sport opportunity for upper- class members in the magnificent Payne Whitney Gymnasium. Hence, as far as I could see as a young instructor, salary increases were just something that happened at the whim of the director (Bob Kiphuth). As I recall, also, when I started at Western Ontario ("Western") in 1949, such "developing portfolios" weren't "all the rage" either. (Nowadays, of course, promotion depends greatly upon one having successive "outside" research grants in your portfolio"!)

Fortunately (for me!), I had "gotten the message" early on from relating to colleagues in certain other departments that "writing and research" was it (!) for university personnel. (However, I soon discovered also that, *after most of them had achieved tenure*, the importance of writing and research declined greatly...) So, building on that "first-olive-out-of-the bottle" publication about human somato-types back in 1948, I had gradually created a detailed listing of publications commencing with my first "sojourn" in Canada and continuing throughout the 1950s decade. However, I did not keep track in the same way of various internal and external professional responsibilities and assignments assumed for that first ten-year period in professional-preparation work. For example, in 1953 I was elected president of a "entity" called "Canadian Directors of Professional Preparation in Physical Education" at a meeting held at the University of Manitoba. Yet today that isn't listed in my present dossier, and there a number of other items omitted back then.

*Note: So I did start to do "just that" (i.e., to enumerate everything of any significance at all after I arrived at The University of Michigan in 1956). I have continued this practice with perhaps too great diligence since. All told there have been 445 articles published up to July, 2012, along with some 57 books and monographs to October, 2012. (See the appendices below.) As well, there is an almost endless list of outside presentations at conferences and "internal involvements" of the type that could be helpful "for display" on the "appropriate" oc- casion. In addition, as of today (2012/11/26), three books have been published this year. So, as it turned out, I have kept a detailed of these "internal" and "external" involvements all these years down to the present. Most of this information is included at the end of the main portion of this autobiography. So, then and there, as it turned out, the only thing left for me to do right now is to construct some sort of a hopefully interesting narrative for the remaining 30 years+ since then. Immediately I knew also that no one in his right mind claiming a semblance of sanity would be inclined to read through these remain- ing single-spaced pages of Earle Zeigler "at work"!*

Returning to my spellbinding autobiographical narrative, including my detailed "accounting of activities", I am back on the page covering the year 1976-77 at the point when I was making up my mind to "cease and desist" being a dean at the end of five years instead of carrying on to fulfill a possible seven-year appointment. Poring over my itemized listing of "everything" that would be happening in regard to trips and presentations in the subsequent 1977-78 academic year, *the proverbial "light bulb" came on over my head just as it does in occasional newspaper cartoons.* Why so? One day in the early months of 1977, I had received word that I had been chosen as the second Alliance Scholar-of-the-Year by the American Alliance for Health, Physical Education, Recreation, and Dance!

Hence the question must have also arisen at that moment of my existence: "How could I, as a active on the "home front" dean, accept this great honor from the official professional *American* organization in my field, an honor that entailed a variety of *prescribed* visitation and presentations all over America in the ensuing year—plus many other invitations of a like nature—*and still be an active dean on the job at Western?*" In addition there were certain worldwide conferences going on that year that I typically would have been obligated to attend anyhow as a "scholarly professor". Looking back, that *must* have been what tipped the scales in the making of my decision to opt out as dean at the end of five years instead of fulfilling the longer seven-year assignment. I was so very fortunate that this five-year option had been available from the very beginning in early 1972. Now, today in 2012, I truly understand how I must have been "glad to 'get out'" of my dean's post— everything considered—*and* also to be able to rationalize my departure ethically and satisfactorily. Yet it *had to be* somewhat of a disappointed as well… "Higher administration" on the Western campus, on the other hand, must have breathed a sigh of relief to get this "intractable" dean out of their hair while on earned administrative leave for a year.

*Note: After I stepped down as dean, it seems that almost "automati- cally" I became active in the Western Faculty Association. This group on any campus is typically in some sort of a confrontation with "higher administration" In fact, after becoming active with this group, I was asked to run for the post of president. It's probably just as well that I lost out by a few votes for this post, one that is truly time demanding! I was told that some votes that I may have lost were probably because some faculty members could not envision a "former dean" being "on the side of " the general faculty. Yet I really was! So, for a couple of years, I served as chair of the committee to which "ag- grieved professors" could come for advice and help with their prob- lems.*

## A Year As a "Traveling Scholar"

Next I checked with my "infallible" historical summary of my manifold "involvements" at my side, between June 14 and 17 of a year of administrative leave thankfully granted me after stepping down as dean at the end of a five-year period. This turned out to be the same year that we traveled all over North America because I had won the Outstanding Scholar Award of the AAHPERD. Right off I had presented two papers in Toronto at the annual convention of the Canadian Association for Health, Physical Education and Recreation. One had to do with sport and physical activity in the Middle Ages; the other was mysteriously called "Relationships in Physical Education: A Viewpoint from History and Philosophy." In retrospect the latter sounds like an historical "gossip column"! Next to my great surprise I discovered as I read my summary that about 10 days later I gave a paper in Madrid, Spain at the International Physical Education and Sport Congress. It was titled "The Fivefold Function of Physical Education and Sport Within Higher Education". I can still recall the standing ovation I received for enlightening my international colleagues on this topic. (*Actually I haven't the slightest recollection of that occasion...*)

Immediately after that, and I do remember this experience on July 6, I enlightened a group of Israeli in Israel (!) with a presentation titled "Reactions to Sport and Physical Activity in Israeli Life within Jewish Culture." Where I acquired the temerity to walk on Israeli soil *for the first time* and tell the citizenry what my reaction to their sport and physical activity was like, I simply do not know... Keeping in mind that this was indeed a "year of liberation"—both an administrative-leave year *and* a year of "servitude" because of the "Scholar Award"—what happened next? Guess what? Bert and I were going to take a trip to Germany! Somehow I was invited, accepted, and then a schedule was arranged for me to speak to present a paper *in German* at a number of German universities. Herbert Haag, Prof. Dr. Haag—as they identify themselves over there—arranged for a number of universities in *Deutschland traveling* from north to south where folks would presumably sit still while I uttered some "timeless words of wisdom to the assembled multitude in their native tongue." So, with some help from two friends (i.e., natives who had emigrated to North America), I polished my presentation-to-be. It was titled "Der Beitrag des Sports und der koerperliche Betaetigung zur Verbesserung der Lebensqualitaet". Translated this says: "Sport and Physical Activity's Contribution to the Improvement of the Quality of Life." (Interestingly, I still have that paper available and, having reread it. I do believe everything I said in it 35 years ago about what a quality program in physical activity and related health education can do for people rings true to this very day! In addition—while I'mstill alive—I'd be delighted to send it to anyone who reads German. Email me at efzeigler@shaw.ca.

So we flew to Germany in early October, rented an ordinary looking car, and drove to Kiel in northern Germany where Dr. Haag was the program director.

After a presentation there, we continued by going south in Germany to visit other universities at Hamburg, Muenster, Ruhr University-Bochum, Bonn, Cologne, Frankfurt, Karlsruhe, Tuebingen, and Munich. (Along the way we deviated slightly when I made a presentation about the status of physical education and sport philosophy in North America at the Free University of Belgium on November 17.)

Looking back, I don't know how the devil we ever managed to pull the whole trip off ! And also, quite frankly, the trip is now only a blur in my mind. The only thing I can remember is that, at some point during my talk in Belgium, the audience laughed at something I said that was *not* intended to be funny. Later I learned that one word I had used in speaking German could also be translated colloquially as "whorehouse." Oh yes, I do remember a bit more about this trip. The day along the way that we arrived in Paris, our rented vehicle wouldn't start when we wanted to leave. So we had to transfer to public transportation for a while. And then (!), when we got back to the airport at the end of the month to fly back home to Illinois, the airport was closed! Its operations were being carried out at another airport many miles away. The airline had not been able to notify us, they said later, because we were moving from town to town throughout Germany. Obviously, receiving this news, we panicked because we had a flight scheduled there in two hours going back to Toronto,—and that departure was *from a different airport hours away*! What to do?

Somehow we got rid of the rented vehicle and then "commandeered" a taxi telling the poor driver what time our flight was scheduled to leave… However, the confident taxi driver said: "Don't worry; I'll get you there in time." So away we went to travel 145 kilometers on the wildest ride I have ever experienced before or since. It took us about two and one half hours of burning up the highway at speeds Bert and I had never traveled before or since! Periodically I would sneak a look at the speedometer that said 120, 130, and once even 140 kilometers an hour. The result: we did get there by 11:00 p.m. for a flight scheduled to depart at 11:30 p.m.. Unfortunately, or perhaps fortunately, we were saved from missing our flight. Hundreds of other people were also there milling around, all wanting to get on the same flight! So a number of us ended up spending the night on very nice, marble (!) benches available, and then got a flight out the next day. (I should add that subsequently the airline very thoughtfully reimbursed me for what I had to pay the taxi driver (including his handsome tip—*Trinkgeld* in German).

After our "German experience", the events of my sabbatical year leading up to the AAHPERD annual convention and the Outstanding Scholar Award continued apace. The first half of 1978 found me presenting papers here and there on the North American continent. Several were in relation to the commitment one had to make *to actually receive* this Scholar-of-the-Year Award. We had brought a Volkswagen "bug" back with us from our earlier visit to Germany; so, we packed that trusty vehicle "to the gills" and drove it all over America in the process of fulfilling my commitment. There were presentations to the University of Maryland, College Park; University of North Carolina, Greensboro; the University of Georgia, Athens; and eight different presentations at institutions within a 60- mile radius of Atlanta (ranging from Morris Brown College to Georgia State University).

Next, also as part of the commitment based on the AAHPERD Award, I visited and made presentations at Washington State University, Pullman, and nearby University of Idaho. The final of the three "official" Alliance Scholar Lectures was made at Southern Illinois University, Carbondale on April 9. However, our "wanderings" were not over yet; I gave the "Murphy Lecture" at Arizona State University, Tempe, on April 19 that was somehow followed by one of my "new directions for the field" talks at San Diego State University on April 21. Then, don't ask me how, on the way back to Tennessee where the annual convention of AAHPERD was scheduled, we stopped briefly to "enchant the multitudes" at the University of New Mexico, Albuquerque on April 27. Why we were also going back to Tennessee, as I recall, was for me to have the opportunity to address the final session of the McKenzie Symposium on Sport on May 5. Then, evidently, to make that journey even more worthwhile, my good friend and former colleague at Illinois, Don Franks, convinced me to stay on and teach a short course on sport and physical education philosophy at the University of Tennessee from May 8 to June 6.

By this time, anyone reading about this succession of involvements here and there all over the place must be thinking: "Doesn't this guy have a home?" I know it seems questionable, but the answer was definitely in the affirmative! Remember that this was just one year out of a lifetime that was carried out in this fashion—and all of this because of the awarding of the *second* annual Scholar of the Year Award in America from the American Alliance. Finally, the academic year of 1977-78 was brought to an end by another paper at the NAPECW-NCPEAM Conference in Denver, Colorado on June 2, and a final presentation of some sort at the University of Connecticut, Storrs on June 13.

To put the icing on the cake during my year of "vacation", I somehow managed to attend the Commonwealth Conference on Sport and Physical Education at the University of Alberta, Edmonton, AB, Canada from July 31 to August 2. But I don't understand it; somehow (!) I can't find any mention of a title for any sort of a presentation there. Was I simply hoarse and worn out and maybe undergoing a period of recovery? Perhaps... But it's more likely that I made a mistake and accidentally omitted listing such a title. However, one less listing was no problem at that point, because promotion in rank was no longer a factor of importance. I was a *full* professor no matter whatever interpretation you may make as to praising or deriding that so-called lofty perch.

*(Note: In Germany, for example, where professors rank highest of all professions in respect in the minds society members, you would (could!) typically place the words "Professor Doktor so-and-so" before your full name at the top of any stationery used. In fact, if you also had been awarded any honorary doctoral degrees, one typically adds one or more "Drs." after his or her name. This means that today I could—if teaching in Germany—call myself "Professor Dr., Dr., Dr., Dr. Earle F. Zeigler"! However, in North America, if in the public sector, I'm lucky if I'm not addressed as "Hey, you!" And when at the local barber shop when it's my turn, it's "Earle; you're next..." C'est la vie...)*

## Resumption of "Life As Usual"

I confess to some confusion with my ongoing narrative at this point. Memories have faded; that's for sure. It's the middle of the year 1978. My "over-the-decades" list of "things done" is propped up next to me appears to have arrived at page 40. (There are actually a total of 86 pages of "similar things" close by.) Just below on *this page here* is the next heading already typewritten that says: "Remarks at 90th

Birthday Party, August 20, 2009! However, as I move along here carefully and studiously, only the "Creator" might be able to designate what the page will be for that heading as I complete this breathtaking tale… This 1978 date means that I have 30+ years of "something" staring me in the face to complete this autobiographical narrative. Okay. However, the problem is not only that I'm running out of gas, so to speak. It is also that I'm quite certain that anyone who might read this doesn't want to read a continuation of where I just left off. So what I must do, I believe, is to "return to earth on the home front."

Yet what do I find there? I'm 59 years old, a dangerous age, and certainly not looking forward to the mandatory retirement at age 65 that was universally mandatory at that time. I was still involved conscientiously doing all of those "things" and making all of those "noises" that a *full* professor should be uttering… I did find actually that I was "in a rut" because the die had been cast for my future!! So, for example, from Oct. 5-7, I went as Member-at-Large to a meeting of the Executive Committee of the Philosophic Society for the Study of Sport in Fort Worth Texas. There I also presented a paper—one *had* to do this, I might add, to get any financial assistance for the trip back at the home front. The paper was titled "Bridging the Gap from One's Sense of Life to Ethical Sport Decisions." *This is still an appropriate topic today as I write these words in 2012.*

Continuing on—I can't believe it. It seems as if I just about got home when I went out that proverbial door again—this time as the invited banquet speaker at the annual meeting of the Mid-American Conference Physical Education Group that was held in Mt. Pleasant, Michigan from Oct. 14-15 of 1978. My banquet topic was "Those Things That Have 'Got to Go' in the Eighties". That same day I note that I conducted a session in a management course there regaling students on the use of the Harvard case method as one technique in the development of administrative competency.

**ENOUGH ALREADY**! This is getting boring even for me who can't remember that he experienced it; so, I can imagine how anyone who hasn't fallen asleep yet must feel. As I look at the side of page 41 in the "endless summation" where I have been taking most of this information from, I note that—by the writing of a preface for the Japanese edition of my physical education and sport philosophy text to be published—that this made a total of 230 articles published! Whom was I competing with? And I must confess that—despite all of this verbiage created—we still don't have universally good programs of physical activity and health education at all levels of education! A further thought: I wonder to what extent we in the field even read what our colleagues have written in the various journals extant...? (The sun is shining outside, but this thought makes it a glum day nevertheless...)

So here I am now, getting fairly close to concluding my "autobiographical opus" in the fall of year 2012, try "dredge up" where I was and what I "was up to" at the beginning of 1979... Because of my commitment to writing and research, and to the field of education overall, I probably didn't make sufficient plans for retirement. However. I was lucky! And this is true, even though I had stumbled along financially until about a year and a half before I retired. At that point, Bert and I really started thinking about retirement. Different strategies loomed in front of us, but we realized that they weren't needed... Why? Because, somehow, each month I receive a number of different checks—not big ones!—of varying sizes and quantities from all of the different universities where I worked and from each country as well.. In addition, as a result of our return to Canada, we didn't have to worry about medical expenses! Of course, you pay something here and there (e.g. isolated medication expense that in my case were minimal), but Canada's health plan was a great help with Bert, my wife, until she passed away in late 1998. I admit that at times it does take longer to get help in Canada, but *if it's a true emergency, you are taken care of right away! America should start taking care of all of its ageing people in the same way!*)

Living in Canada now, and having become a citizen in 1984 after moving here for the second time in 1971, there is no way I could bring myself to return to America. I confess to having become very disappointed about the "country of my birth." They crow about their lofty value system, but somehow, and most sadly so, I have again come to the conclusion that "talking a good game" isn't the same thing as "putting those values into practice". I do pay taxes and vote in both countries (i.e., only for president in America through the State of Washington). Frankly, as a type of "refugee," I live here because I "like the climate better". That statement undoubtedly sounds a bit odd because Canada is said to be "the land of ice, snow, Inuits, and people who speak French," However, I live in the lower mainland of British Columbia where that white stuff is a distinct rarity, and you'd do somewhat better speaking Chinese than French! It does rain more than occasionally, I must admit. In addition, I do like another kind of "climate" much better! In this sense I am referring to the overall way of life I enjoy and what Canada is doing in relation to what Canada says that it "stands for"…

This is not to say that we don't have problems up here. In BC alone, we have 100 native Indian tribes (now known as nations) that are distributed geographically throughout the province. I keep telling my grandson that he'd be better off eventually living somewhere else than here. Why? Because only one land claim by one aboriginal tribe (nation!) has been settled by the Province of BC. After the other 99 settlements are consummated, there won't be any room for the rest of BC's "out-of-hand", multi-ethnic population to sit down—or even to have enough money to move and enjoy life elsewhere. That is an exaggeration, I confess…

When I said above that I liked the climate in Canada better, that was a play on words too. What I really meant was that I find Canada a country in which its present beliefs and social philosophy seem much better than those operative in America as it is presently constituted *and* functioning. For example, I am very upset about the fact that the United States became the first country in the 21st century to defy the United Nations by waging war against Iraq ostensibly to oust an evil dictator. I know that he was a tyrant who oversaw many terrible acts by his sons and other henchmen. But that's not the point. America has set a terrible precedent in a highly troubled world by its action. (I must point oat that Canada did not approve this almost unilateral action.) And there's one more vital point. All of those Iraqi citizens and solders, not to mention fine American soldiers, male and female were betrayed! How so? The world was lied to by American and British political leaders! Saddam did not have the nuclear weapons of destruction that were ascribed to him! (Shades of Vietnam and the 50,000 Americans and endless number of Vietnamese who died to hold back the forces of communism!

Ha!) And what or who was next? I recall when my television set announced—some years ago now—that George "W" was going to step up the United States' long-standing effort to democratize the world. Egad! "Who's next" in the parade of countries the U.S. is determined to democratize (or whatever!) while exporting capitalism, technology, and Christianity as well? As it turned out, the answer was "Afghanistan". However, such conquest is turning out to be a "sticky wicket", actually a "disaster". The Afghanistan incursion has deteriorated to the point where some Afghan soldiers are shooting their American counterparts who are training them to defend their own country. This is beyond belief !) America should just "declare victory" and move on to "bigger and better things." I'm beginning to wonder what Iran will look like after a nuclear bomb is dropped on it by either America or Israel? Stand by…

For a second example of the prevailing climate that disturbs me in the United States, let me move to an area where I worked professionally for another example. Having taught, administered, and periodically coached sport, physical education, and recreation programs at Yale, Michigan, and Illinois also, I can speak authoritatively about sport in general and even more specifically about the intercollegiate athletics scene in the United States of America. Sport in the Ivy League and similar institutions (categorized as Division 3, NCAA) is typically just fine. It is doing quite well what it's intended to do. However, athletics in all of those other universities where gate receipts is a vital factor (i.e., NCAA Division I and II universities), the situation has gradually but steadily throughout the entire 20th century gotten completely out of hand. It is semi-professional, in some cases actually professional! Moreover, this fact has occasioned all of the attendant vices that have crept into such programs when sponsored by educational institutions. Educational values in respect to these participants have been gradually and increasingly "decimated" since the beginning of the 20th century.

The entire, unfortunate development in commercialized, competitive sport that developed gradually throughout the 20th century is symptomatic of the entire society. My position about this aspect of society is this: "Sport was created by humans to serve humans beneficially." Serve beneficially, yes; however, it seems now that many professional and semi-professional athletes—not to mention the situation in overly emphasized high school sport competition—are there to serve what has be a most undesirable "sport goliath" with dollar bills stuffed in all of the "creature's" pockets and various orifices. It is accompanied and insidiously goaded by a mindless public watching with vicarious, often rapturous involvement. All of this is akin to the seduction of the populace that occurred in ancient Rome. Sadly, while this is taking place, the overwhelming majority of children and young people is getting a poor (or no!) introduction to what ought to be a fine program of health instruction, physical activity education, and physical recreation (including intramural athletic competition) in the public schools and related institutions. *Not only are "the rich getting richer, and the poor poorer," the elite athletes are getting the attention, and "normal" and "challenged" youngsters are getting inadequate programming—and fatter in the process!*

Once again, this is not to say that Canada has no problems. The situation now is such that university programs in our field claim to be disciplinary programs rather than professional-preparation programs. We don't train teachers any more in the specific university department. Now we just train people in the disciplinary nature of the field that formerly downtrodden physical educators increasingly might soon call kinesiology or human kinetics to improve their status. If any of these students want to continue on with professional preparation, and then get a license to teach within public education, *they work with the physical and health education department of a faculty of education!* Personally, therefore, I've tried to maintain both the professional and disciplinary relationships. Unfortunately, the "professional component" of our field is making only very faint noises these days...

Looking to the future after I was dubbed "emeritus" in 1989, my wife (Bert) and I decided to divide the year into four parts. In the fall, we planned to be in London, Ontario, where we had a town house. During January and February, we wanted to go where it was a little warmer, perhaps to San Diego or Florida. The only thing other than "wherewithal" that I wanted to take with me was my portable computer! (This item was a "companion" that Bert wasn't very excited to have accompanying us!) In the spring, we decided to return to London, Ontario to get ready for income tax time. (Ugh!) As a dual citizen, I must file on both sides of the border, and it is typically highly confusing. Spring is also conference season in our field, and I wanted to continue with the Academy (now the NAK), the AAHPERD, sport history, sport management, and also to attend every two years the meeting of the International Society for Comparative Physical Education and Sport. In addition, PHE Canada, formerly the Canadian Association for HPER, still meets annually.

*(Note: I eventually had to cut back somewhere because going to so many meetings requires a lot of money. Luckily, we were able to cope because the department helped out. Also, I tell the Canadian govern- ment that I'm self-employed part time— which I am—and thus I can deduct certain expenses on my tax returns. However, they may "close in on me" because now my business expenses typically significantly exceed any incoming royalties.*

## "Where Do We Go From Here?"

Life for Bert and me settled down as we achieved "senior—citizen status" (ha!). As we looked forward to x number of years in retirement (i.e., really the semi- retirement I aspired for me), we had to make a decision about the best location in which to spend our "golden years." We knew that we didn't want to move close to Don and Brannon north of New York City. Of course, we wanted to keep in touch with Don as much as possible, however, Brannon and Bert didn't hit it off at all originally. As soon as Brannon moved into Don's domain, examples of Barbara's artwork began to disappear or were draped over with a shawl (or whatever). (I could understand that it didn't "mesh" with their décor, of course.) In addition, we had had such a great relationship with Emily, Don's first wife, of whom we "thought the world." We just did not understand what had happened with what we thought had been such a "great relationship".

So the obvious choice for us was to explore the idea of a move to western Canada to be near Barbara, our daughter. We began to explore the possibility of another move. Most fortunately we came up with an ideal solution. There was a development known as Sudden Valley on Lake Whatcom next to Bellingham, Washington just south of the American-Canadian border. It had everything that we had ever dreamed of as a desirable place to live climate wise and facilities & arrangements wise—and it was affordable! So we devised what turned out to be an excellent arrangement: we would spend three-month segments of our time in each place depending on the time of the year. That meant that winter would spent out west, spring in Ontario, summer in Sudden Valley on the lake, and the fall season back in London, Ontario again. This blissful arrangement extended for six years, certainly a most happy time in our lives!

As we were aging, of course,, we then decided that the time had come to settle down in one place! Most fortunately we were able to purchase an ideal condominium in a set-up known as Queens-Gate Complex in Richmond, British Columbia that was about a mile away from daughter Barbara's home. Not only was it a premium property, there was also a swimming pool and gymnasium. So, folks, we had the ideal arrangement for weekend sojourns on Lake Whatcom so long as we could get across the border into the States without too many inordinate hold-ups. (In retrospect, we really did enjoy "the Sudden Valley Experience" in all respects. I have asked Anne and Barbara to arrange after my death for ½ of my ashes to be joined with Bert's at our favorite lakeside spot.)

*Note: As life "home on the range" moved along very nicely, I should say that I have spared you, my reader (are you still there?), a good ten years of information about my many presentations, articles, and books. Aren't you pleased about the consideration I have shown you? However, never fear! At this point it is 1990, and I must beg your indulgence again by recapturing the "special recognitions" that I received from my American colleagues at the end of the 1980s.*

## Special Recognitions for Professional Service

In 1996 Bert and I decided that flying back and forth from east to west (and vice versa) every three months for six years was beginning to wear a bit thin. So we made "the big decision" to leave London, Ontario forever. It was sad in a way to do so, because London had welcomed us twice: once as a young family in 1949 starting out on a new adventure in a "foreign" country—and then again when I became completely disenchanted with Illinois and America in 1968 after the Illinois slush-fund scandal broke (described above). Hence, "moving" was "the thing to do" at that point, and we did it!

Once again, we were most fortunate. The money from the townhouse we sold back in London, plus about $50,000 more gave us enough to buy a very nice condo at 105-8560 General Currie Rd., in Richmond, BC for $199,000 in 1996. It is known as Queen's Gate, the first "luxury" condo of its type built in Richmond and—happy day!—it had a very nice, small swimming pool and gym that I have used quite regularly ever since. Bert used to enjoy swimming in it as well. So here we were in 1996 successfully relocated in a very nice condo about 1 and ½ miles away from Barbara's home. (Little did we know at the time that just about all of the condominiums built in the area at the time had significant deficiencies due to an inadequate building format approved by the federal government.

All sorts of nice "other things" happened in that eighth decade of my life. I had, of course, not foreseen any of them. I don't want to bore you, my faithful reader (i.e., if indeed you have gotten this far!); so I will simply list briefly the various types of recognition that I received at a variety of occasions. It was just as "Decade #8" was coming into view that the North American Society for Sport Management (a professional association that I and others had help to start in 1986) decided to establish an annual **Earle F. Zeigler Lecture.** So, in 1989 I was invited me to present the first such lecture at NASSM's annual meeting. My wordy title

for this address was "Using History to Explain What to Avoid and What to Do As We Face an Uncertain Future". Then in September of 1989, since I would be concluding a four-year, part-time extension of my employment at Western that was arranged by Dean Bert Taylor, a decision was made to hold a retirement affair for me titled **The Earle F. Zeigler Symposium on Current Issues in Physical Education.**

Next, just as we moved into the 1990s, I received word that I was to receive *the highest award* of the American Alliance for Health, Physical Education, Recreation and Dance at its General Session on March 29, 1990. This consisted of **The Luther Halsey Gulick Medal** that is named after an early leader of the Alliance. All in all that was quite a day, especially since it been preceded the previous year by my receipt of **The Hetherington Award of the National Academy of Kinesiology** (its highest award).

In October of 1991, I was inducted into ***Western's Hall of Wrestling Fame.*** This recognition was based on my service as wrestling coach starting in 1952-53 when Western won the inter-university championship of what amounted to "central" Canada.

Then in April of 1994, I was named as the first ***Human Movement Sciences and Education Distinguished Scholar*** at Memphis State University in Memphis, Tennessee. My address was titled "Trends in Transition: The Allied Professions Look to the 21st Century. April 27, 1994.

Next I was inducted in ***Western University's "W" Club Hall of Fame (Builder Category)*** in October of 1995.

Following this, I received a ***Doctor of Science degree (D.Sc.) from University of Lethbridge*** in May 1997.

Finally, I was inducted into ***The Swimming Wall of Honour at Western University*** on October 20, 2000. I was the first swimming coach there in 1949-50. Then I took over as wrestling coach in 1952-53 when the coach left. However, I returned to become swimming coach again in 1954-55 when I was needed there.

## Fate Steps In

Life was just fine at that point; the future looked bright. And then one day in late January of 2008, our young grandson, Kenan, became ill. Cold or flu? Who knew? At any rate, Barbara left him in our care since she had to go to work. Later that day she picked him up on the way home and away they went. During that evening Bert said she didn't feel too well; so, we assumed she had caught his cold. (I should explain that Bert's immunity was low because of her earlier lung operation that I mentioned before.) We went to bed and, about five a.m., Bert got up to go to the bathroom. Then I heard a "thud" coming from the end of the bed! She had collapsed to the floor! What to do? I shut the window, put a blanket over her, and called 911. Nearby Richmond Hospital dispatched an ambulance that arrived promptly and took her away. I dressed and followed her by car a.s.a.p.

When I got to the hospital about a mile away, she was settled in comfortably waiting for a room assignment.

Sadly things went from bad to worse, and the next thing we knew Bert was in a really bad way with pneumonia—and on a respirator. The next five days are a blur now. Don flew out from New York City hurriedly, but then had to return to teach his law classes. Barbara and I were in an out of the hospital for a period of five days! Finally, the attending physician said: "The time has come to take out the respirator to see if she can breathe on her own without it." She couldn't... So, with Barbara on one side of the bed holding Bert's right hand, and I on the other holding the left, Bert passed away quietly at age 81 on February 5, 1998—a very sad time... We had been together since we started "going steady" at Bates College toward the end of our sophomore year (1937-38). We had had our "ups and downs" from day #1, but all in all it was a *most* successful marriage. I could not have asked for a better helpmate and partner. Our two children had had an absolutely devoted mother! Bert's surprise death was indeed a tragedy!

Life eventually returned to semi-normal after that. I was in "our" condo with Bert's ashes in a container by the fireplace. The plan was that they would be intermingled with mine at a "later date" and cast into Lake Whatcom at a favorite spot where we used to sit afternoons on nice days close to our condo in Sudden Valley... (Now they're stored with Barbara at her home.) I didn't know quite what to do. I couldn't see myself living alone for long. Fortunately a good friend of ours for many years, Bonnie Youngberg, decided to arrange a trip to Alaska and suggested that I go with her. Great idea—and away we went in early July on 1998. To save money the idea was that we would share a room... This worked out fine; we had a great time—with no "friendly encounters," however.

## I Meet Anne Rogers!

Just after Bert died so tragically on February 5, 1998, British Columbia had a problem of significant magnitude. Its Lower Mainland's had a so-called "leaky-condo crisis" that soon was in full swing. It turned out that literally thousands of condominiums supposedly built according to governmental standards turned out to be grossly deficient. A number of us weren't thrilled with the way our elected

condo council was handling the situation—not that we could do any better...
Someone asked me if I wanted to become a member of an informal group that
eventually termed itself "The Underground Council". A nice lady with a great
sense of humor, Phyllis Craib, even got us a meeting with the original real estate
developer of our leaky condo. On our "Council" I very soon discovered, also,
an attractive, most personable lady living in a condo just two doors down the
hall from me. I soon learned that her name was Anne Rogers. We had occasionally exchanged "hellos" previously, because her car was typically parked just two
spaces down from mine in our underground garage.

Humorously, just at the time when Anne and I discovered that we would like
to be more than just "friends," it happened that a trip had been planned, and I
was going out the door with our old friend Bonnie Youngberg "from back east"
to spend a week in Alaska. And we would be together sharing one room for the
entire experience. I'm sure Anne didn't know what to think... What I was thinking was that my upcoming "Alaskan experience" would have to be an absolutely
Platonic one! It was, most fortunately, and I was honestly able to resume a court-
ship with Anne on my return. Anne and I really seemed to "hit it off " and "got
along famously" thereafter during the next few months. I well remember propos-
ing to her poolside in Sudden Valley, Bellingham on a sunny day early that fall
of 2008. We were married on February 27, 1999 surrounded by Barbara and
friends from the Vancouver area. Then we all enjoyed a delightful luncheon in a
Vancouver hotel followed by a night in the bridal suite for two. A great day!

After mutual planning, Anne took early retirement from the B.C. Compensation
Board, but continued part time as a practicing nurse. She sold her condo and
moved into mine. Somehow we achieved a "consolidation" of our furnishings
with "overages and excesses" going in the direction of daughter Barbara close
by for acceptance or rejection. At the same time, arrangements were made about
the possibility of my demise (e.g., powers of attorney, "fair" distribution of pos-
sessions) so that the interests of all three parties (Anne, Don, and Barbara) were
considered. I doubt very much if anyone—including me—thought that I would
be writing these words some 12 plus years later...

## Remarks at 90th Birthday Party on August 20, 2009

First, I thank all of you who have made the effort to be here today. Considering the trials and tribulations of travel these days—including border-crossing restrictions—I was successful in keeping colleagues from New York City and Tempe, Arizona at home with their families. I must thank as well those faraway, good friends who were kind and thoughtful enough to write me letters that made an old man "feel good."

*"EFZ" at his 90ᵗʰ Birthday Party*

Next I thank my wonderful wife, Anne Rogers, for undertaking this birthday project with help from my daughter, Barbara. On February 27, Anne and I celebrated 12 extremely happy and fulfilling years together. We achieved this by starting out with one premise as a daily motto: "What can I do to make my partner's life happy and fulfilling?" This formula worked! Excuse me for taking a minute to thank all the people who helped me along the way. I must make special mention of my mother and grandparents—and even my stepfather whose most conservative stances drove me early on to comprehend what I stand for today.

I must mention my late wife, Bert Bell Zeigler. We were together through "thick and thin" for 61 years all together. She deserves "full credit for keeping the show on the road" and especially for our two children as "end products." I am also very proud of my daughter, Barbara Zeigler, an art professor at UBC, and my deceased son, Donald, who was an outstanding law professor at New York Law School.

I'm so very glad to be alive and here today. As a matter of fact, I'm glad to be anywhere! When you get to age 93, if you wake up in the morning at my 90th Birthday Party in the lounge in our condominium I am finding that it's somewhat easier to get older than it is to get wiser. The pace of life seems to be increasing, also. However, it's not the pace of life that worries me; it's just that upcoming sudden stop at the end…

How does one know when he's getting old? I got to think about this question, and I think I have a few "corny" answers.

"OLD" IS WHEN… Your sweetie says, "Let's go upstairs and make love," and you answer, "Pick one, I can't do both!"

Or "OLD" IS WHEN… You don't care where your spouse goes, just as long as you don't have to go along.

Or "OLD" IS WHEN… "Getting a little action" means I don't need to take any fiber today.

Or "OLD" IS WHEN… "Getting lucky" means you found your car in the parking lot.

Or "OLD" IS WHEN… An "all-nighter" means not getting up to go to the bathroom. Ha!

So much for getting old. I also do worry about the world in the future. Some say the world is lost. Others don't agree. However, if it's not lost, where is it? That is a good question, but don't worry, I'm not going to pontificate on that unbelievably complex matter.

However, I do want to pontificate a moment on what I consider to be the two burning issues related to my professional pursuits over the past 70+ years. I am greatly concerned about the fact that the large majority of "normal" and "special needs" children and youth are not getting a quality physical activity and related health education program (including intramural athletics) that would help them live life more fully now and in the future— and actually help them live longer as well.

Further, and this factor has a direct relationship to my first issue, I strongly believe that highly competitive sport may actually be doing more harm to the world than good! Somehow, the more sport is professionalized as a result of globalism, capitalism, and technology, the more its potential beneficial impact on society declines. Sport has become a reflection of a society that has been influenced unfavorably by these developments. The ideals of honesty, sportsmanship, good will, and fair play are threatened daily.

I must bring these thoughts to a close. My friends, I must tell you that I'll try hard to keep up my enthusiasm for the 90s—if such is to be the case. It is difficult, though.

The other day I was sitting in a rocking chair, and I had to ask

Anne to help me get it going…

I think I know all the answers. But nobody wants to ask me questions any more…!

I leave you with those immortal words by that famous

18th-19th century German literary figure, Johann Wolfgang von Goethe. "Es irrt den Mensch solang er strebt." No one ever figured out exactly what he meant with that thought. No, seriously, these stirring words drilled into me by my favorite German professor, Sammy Harms at Bates College, were translated as "The human errs, but strive he must."

Satchell Page, the legendary Black baseball pitcher caught the spirit of Goethe's exhortation, in these more understandable words:

> "DON'T LOOK BACK—AND DON'T REST ON YOUR OARS—
> THEY'RE GAINING ON YOU!

Finally, we look forward to an uncertain future. The world has many problems, and we **OURSELVES** must solve them if this "noble experiment" is to succeed. The odds don't look good.

We can only look forward to the "era of Obama" and hope that humans of intelligence and good will can make it work. Obama's task may seem hopeless, but we simply must give him every chance to succeed.

In closing I want to thank my Grandson Kenan and his associates for today's musical entertainment.

Thank you, one and all, for making this day such a happy one for Anne and me.

## The "Last Best Hope" on Earth?

Because my feelings will undoubtedly "break through" soon in this autobiographical effort, I must say at the outset that I am especially disturbed about what is happening in (or to) America. I believe that, as the world's only superpower now, the U.S.A.—supposedly "The Last Best Hope of Earth" is (and has been!) increasingly playing a negative role with its international efforts over the years! This is my belief as well intentioned as it claims it is and may indeed be in particular instances.

I believe that this has happened because a "substantive part" of America has been "almost unconsciously" disintegrating within from the standpoint of human values! I just happened to have been born a citizen of that country that was once supposed to be that "last best hope on earth." Now the "last best hope" is that the rest of the world through the power and influence of an now-impotent United Nations will somehow be able to persuade America to fulfill its avowed purpose and stay in its proper place. But who's willing to bet on that possibility?

I explained in the preface that I had simply decided to say "Goodbye" to America! Why? Because I found a new home in Canada! I left America, the land of my birth, because the position in my profession that I wanted simply was not available in America under the educational conditions that I could accept! Of course, you (the reader) might respond: "Who hasn't become concerned about various unsavory developments taking place here and there all over the world? And, moreover, so what that your concern extends to what is happening in your field of endeavor within education?"

All that I can say in reply that you, my reader, are living in a dream world if you don't get involved and learn the facts! My professional endeavor became a calling that I've pursued for 70 years. And what's really discouraging, also, is that my continuing scholarly output of books, monographs and articles will, quite probably, not have any effect on the two destructive aspects or societal developments taking place in my field of physical activity education and what I like to call "educational sport".

Personally I can argue that I've been somewhat of a "winner" in life personally and professionally. However, the field of physical activity education and educational sport to which I've devoted my entire professional life (i.e., the past 70+ years is a "loser"! As I see it, it is in big trouble! And more recently we seem to be "losing out" more than ever in our struggle as professional educators. Some of this "loss" is our fault, of course (e.g., too many jocks with a ball where their brain should reside—male and female!). In the first place, only a minority of children and youth are getting the type of quality program that I deem to be adequate physical activity education with appropriate related health and safety information. Secondly, competitive sport—both in the public sector and within the educational establishment—is increasingly becoming a pawn of an overly capitalistic, nationalistic, and so-called democratic Western world. As it happened, most of the problem really lies with the gradual societal development in the 20th century down to the present. And America, I regret to say, does indeed share a lot of the blame for the shape that the entire world finds itself in.

Despite what I have just said, I am personally living most happily in Canada—but as a dual citizen, an American-Canadian if you will. (I should have called book "Life on the Border Line", as suggested by my friend, John Loy.) However, I have found it best for me personally to desert the United States literally as well as in my heart and mind. Hence I'm one version of "refugee" that we read about in the press. Conversely, the "official American stance," of course, would have you believe that the abiding spirit and practices of "Old Glory"—if only accepted and proclaimed loudly and persistently—are the answer for all of the world's ills. Yet I have gradually but steadily become increasingly disenchanted about what today in reality has become merely an idle boast. The country of my birth appears to actually be a large part of the world's problem in a variety of ways! In essence, as I see it, it is a question of "values loudly espoused, but values *negated* in the final analysis if one 'looks closely'."

The resultant struggle confronting me personally was first to accede to those who say: "Hey, you've done your share. Relax, and let others who follow 'carry the torch' in your field of physical activity education and educational sport. And let's face it: professional sport is professional sport! Get over it. It's money that's 'calling the shots'! And next, my friend, don't become a 'bitter, contradictory old fart' believing blindly that the great United States is over the top of the hill and proceeding apace downward on the backside. Moreover, you shouldn't be so despairing about the future of our entire world (Earth!) because of overpopulation and ongoing degradation of this wonderful, but difficult, environment within which we as still developing creatures that emerged originally million of years ago." To date my response to these good folk is "Forget it"!

Naively I had thought "the world" would be a better place for all people by the turn of the 21ˢᵗ century—by the time I retired! However, because for so many different reasons it doesn't seem to be heading in that direction, I am forced to conclude:

1. That in many ways we are confused about what our values are at the present,

2. That we need to reconsider them and then re-state exactly what we believe they are in light of the changing times, and, finally,

3. That we will then need to assess more carefully—on a regular basis—whether we are living up to those values we finally choose and then so often glibly have glibly espoused with insufficient commitment to bring them to pass.

However, once again, I'm getting ahead of myself with the story about a former kid from East Elmhurst in the Borough of Queens, a part of New York City. Somehow this "kid" is still kicking around at the age of 93 writing these words late one night after a workout in the small gym on the first floor of the condominium in which he lives in Richmond, British Columbia, Canada! How the hell I ended up in western Canada is the essence of some of these "immortal words" that follow. Any comprehensive talk about how the world, its citizens—including me—did or did not screw up, follows on perhaps too many pages. Various opinions about values achieved or aborted have been introduced here and there in this "autobiographical blunderbuss".

In retrospect, it feels like I have been "on the move" ever since I was born in New York City in 1919. My "final move"—other than when "my remains to be sprinkled and thrown to the winds in two places" actually get to the intended destinations—was probably to 105—8560 General Currie Rd. In Richmond,

British Columbia, Canada V6Y 1M2. It is here where I am entering these words on my Mac computer. One of these final "resting places" where my ashes will be thrown to the wind is in Lake Whatcom, Bellingham, Washington, where Bert (Bell Zeigler) and I spent many most pleasant afternoons near our condo before she passed away on Feb. 5, 1998. (The resting place for the other half of my ashes has yet to be determined by Anne [Rogers] and me. Anne and I married in 1999 and have been living "most happily thereafter.")

In 1990 Bert—my late wife of about 60 years—and I bought a condo in Bellingham when we first started to move west from London, Ontario, Canada. We began to live there on an "every-other-season" basis first (i.e., three months in London and three months in Bellingham when the weather was most appropriate). We moved to our Richmond BC permanent residence (a condo!) in 1996 to be near our daughter (Barbara Zeigler), who "professes" in the fine arts department at The University of British Columbia and our grandson, Kenan, who is laboring here and there as a jazz drummer at present. (I had no desire whatsoever at that point to move to the New York City area where my son, Don Zeigler, was a law professor at the New York Law School. (Sadly, even after a double-lung transplant, Don passed away in October of 2011 suffering from the effects of lung cancer).

As I reflect on my present situation, in a literal sense as I said a few pages back, *I am indeed a "refugee" from the United States.* I say this because—for what I believed to be sufficient reason—we decided to move back to Canada permanently in 1971. This will be explained clearly later. We had been here from 1949 to 1956, I as a professor and department head at The University of Western Ontario (now Western University). However, as it turned out, I finally became a citizen here in Canada in 1985 when the America permitted dual citizenship for the first time. (Bert wouldn't think of the idea of becoming a dual citizen…)

How did this happen? Well, frankly, if I were to remain honest with myself, I had no other choice. *I simply could not be involved any longer with a university that annually "sold its soul" in the realm of intercollegiate athletics!* Additionally, no Ivy-League institution where athletics was in its rightful place offered professional preparation in my field as a possible "out" for me! It had come to the point that I could not stomach the situation in intercollegiate athletics at the University of Illinois, UIUC any longer (I was actually getting a stomach ulcer!). My field of physical (activity) education was being disgraced by a "performance ethic" in athletics that was out of control—i.e., do almost "anything" to win in several gate-receipt sports.

This situation came to a head when three professor/coaches involved part time in my department, who also were attached primarily to intercollegiate athletics a related unit on campus, were caught cheating in various ways with selected athletes on their teams (i.e., illegal funding, coaches "swapping grades", etc.).

When news of the scandal broke, all of this disgusting mess was shifted peremptorily to the President's Office, and—believe it or not—I as department head couldn't even find out anything (!) about what was going on in regard to the status of these miscreants who were members of my own staff ! Eventually the three coaches were fired, and the University was penalized somewhat by the Big Ten Conference. And as ridiculous as it seems, the local Champaign-Urbana community held a banquet on behalf of these men and even presented their wives with bejeweled watches! On top of this, there was also a subsequently aborted effort to have statues of the men created to be located prominently in a civic park!

*(Note: I should explain that today faculty members in kinesiology/ physical education units on these campuses are prone to correctly say: "We don't have anything to do with them any more; they're over there!)*

Hence, as a result of this type of a higher-administration, in—bondage situation, I bowed out of my administrative post and remained as a professor in the department. This in itself was extremely disappointing, because at the time our undergraduate and graduate academic programs were undoubtedly rated with the very best in the country. In addition, there had been the possibility of my moving up from being department head to become dean of the College of Physical Education in the near future when Dean McCristal retired. However, in 1971 I finally just "gave up" on Illinois—*and on America!*—and decided to accept a position as dean of a new college (i.e., faculty) at The University of Western Ontario in London, Ontario, Canada. There I knew the athletes in my (our) classes would be bona fide students and that interuniversity athletics was grounded in a sound educational perspective. (In further retrospect, I might have been "best off " to remain "just a professor" in whichever country I settled, because "cognoscenti" have discovered that administrative posts typically leave much to be desired too!)

Finally, to summarize, I have now completed my 93rd year. I am most happy personally because I am married to a wonderful person (Anne Rogers). We are living "the good life" in all respects. I do feel good intrinsically, also, about what I have been able to accomplish both professionally and in a scholarly way. Nevertheless the field of physical activity education is still struggling in a variety of ways, and excesses and malfeasance in both so-called educational sport and professional sport abound. Sadly, what is happening in America is that a large majority of children and youth are receiving *fair, poor, or no* quality program of physical activity and health education (including intramural athletics) *and* the underlying philosophical orientation related to competitive sport places far too much emphasis on "winning as the only thing"!

## PART V

# Counteracting America's Value Orientation

## Introduction

The term *"modernism"* is used to describe cultural movements in today's world that were caused by developing science, technology, and economic globalization. It is said to have started in the late nineteenth and early twentieth century. Conversely, *postmodernism*, as variously defined, can be described loosely as an effort by some intelligent and possibly wise people to react against what is happening to this *modern* world as it "races headlong" toward an indeterminate future.

It can be argued reasonably that America's thrust is modernistic to the nth degree. To the extent that this is true, I am arguing here conversely that Canada should work to counteract America's value orientation as the world moves on into the 21st century. I believe that Canada can—and should do this—by adopting a position that might be called "moderate" postmodernism.

Granted that it will be most difficult for Canada to consistently exhibit a different "thrust" than its neighbor to the south. Nevertheless I believe that now is the time for Canada to create a society characterized by the better elements of what has been termed postmodernism. In fact, I feel Canadians will be *forced* to grapple with the basic thrust of modernism in the 21st century if they hope to avoid the "twilight" that is descending on "American culture" (Berman, 2000). You, the reader, may well question this stark statement. However, bear with me, and let us begin.

What is postmodernism? While most philosophers have been "elsewhere engaged" for the past 50 plus years, what has been called postmodernism, and what I believe is poorly defined, has gradually become a substantive factor in broader intellectual circles. I freely admit to have been grumbling about the term "postmodern" for decades. I say this because somehow it too has been used badly as have other philosophic terms such as existentialism, pragmatism, idealism, realism, etc. as they emerged as common parlance.

In this ongoing process, postmodernism was often used by a minority to challenge prevailing knowledge, and considerably less by the few truly seeking to analyze what was the intent of those who coined the term originally. For example, I am personally not suggesting, as some have, that scientific evidence and empirical reasoning are to be taken with a grain of salt based on someone's subjective reality. Further, if anything is worth saying, I believe it should be said as carefully and understandably as possible. Accordingly, the terms used must be defined, at least tentatively. Otherwise one can't help but think that the speaker (or writer) is either deceitful, a confused person, or has an axe to grind.

Some say that postmodernists claim that nothing in the world is absolute, and that one value is as good as another in a world increasingly threatened with collapse and impending doom. If this were so, then one idea is possibly as good as another as the search goes on to cope with the planet's myriad problems. This caricature of a postmodern world, as one in which we can avoid dealing with the harsh realities facing humankind, is hardly what any rational person might suggest. Despite David Brooks' explanation (*The New York Times*, Aug. 1, 2008)) that "globosclerosis" is keeping the world from united action to solve its major problems, how can humankind choose to avoid (1) looming environmental disaster, (2) ongoing war because of daily terrorist threats, and (3) hordes of displaced, starving people, many of whom are now victims of conflicts within troubled cultures? Further, as we still occasionally hear said, what rational being would argue that one idea is really as good as another?

What then is humankind to do in the face of the present confusion and often conflicted assertions about postmodernism from several quarters that have been bandied about? First, I think we need to consider the world situation as carefully as we possibly can. *Perhaps this will provide us with a snapshot of the milieu where we can at least see the need for a changing (or changed) perspective that would cause humankind to abandon the eventual, destructive elements of modernism that threaten us.* An initial look at some of the developments of the second half of the twentieth century may provide a perspective from which to judge the situation.

## America's Position in the 21st Century

Reviewing America's position in the 21st century may help us to get to the heart of the matter about where the world is heading. For example, we could argue that North Americans do not fully comprehend that their unique position in the history of the world's development will in all probability change radically for the worse in the 21st century. Actually, of course, the years ahead are really going to be difficult ones for all of the world's citizens. However, it does appear that the United States is currently setting itself up "big time" for all kinds of societal difficulties. As the one major nuclear power, Uncle Sam has taken on the ongoing, overriding problem of maintaining large-scale peace. At the turn of the 20th century Teddy Roosevelt, while "speaking softly," nevertheless had his "big stick." The George ("W") Bush administration at the beginning of the 21st century had its "big stick", also, but it didn't give a minute's thought about "speaking softly." The president actually did claim that America's assertive actions were "under God" and were designed for the good of all humanity. This has caused various countries, both large and small, to speak out about many perceive as a bullying posture. Some of these countries may or may not have nuclear arms capability already. That is what is so worrisome.

America, despite all of its proclaimed good intentions, may well find that history is going against it in several ways. This means that previous optimism may need to be tempered to shake politicians loose from delusions, some of which persist despite what seems to be commonsense logic. For example, it is troublesome that, despite the presence of the United Nations, the United States has persisted in positioning itself as the world superpower. Such posturing and aggression, often by unilateral action with the hoped-for, belated sanction of the United Nations, has resulted in the two recent United States-led wars in the Middle East and other incursion into Somalia for very different reasons. There are also other similar situations on the recent horizon (e.g., Afghanistan, the former Yugoslavia, Rwanda, Sudan, and Haiti, respectively). I haven't even mentioned the "Vietnam disaster" of the 1960s, nor the latest incursions into Iraq and Afghanistan. And—let's face it!—who knows what the Central Intelligence Agency has been doing lately to make the world safe for American-style democracy. . .? Cuba, they seemed to have overlooked you lately!

There was reason. post-George "W" that is, to expect selected U.S. cutbacks brought on by today's excessive world involvement and enormous debt. Of course, any such retrenchment would inevitably lead to a decline in the economic and military influence of the United States. But who can argue logically that the present uneasy balance of power is a healthy situation looking to the future? More than a generation ago, Norman Cousins sounded just the right note when he wrote: "the most important factor in the complex equation of the future is the way the human mind responds to crisis." The world culture as we know it today simply must respond adequately and peacefully to the many challenges with which it is being confronted. The societies and nations must individually and collectively respond positively, intelligently, and strongly if humanity as we have known it is to survive.

Additionally, problems and concerns of varying magnitude abound. It seems inevitable that all of the world will be having increasingly severe ecological problems, not to mention the ebbs and flows of an energy crisis. Generally, also, there is a worldwide nutritional problem, and an ongoing situation where the rising expectations of the underdeveloped nations, including their staggering debt, will have to be met somehow. These are just a few of the major concerns looming on the horizon. And, wait a minute, now we find that America has spent so much more "straightening out" the "enemy" that its debt has reached such staggering proportions that paying it off is impossible!

In his highly insightful analysis, *The twilight of American culture* (2000), Morris Berman explained that historically four factors are present when a civilization is threatened with collapse:

(1) Accelerating social and economic inequality,

(2) Declining marginal returns with regard to investments in organizational solutions to socioeconomic problems,

(3) Rapidly dropping levels of literacy, critical understanding, and general intellectual awareness, and

(4) Spiritual death—that is, Spengler's classicism: the emptying out of cultural content and the freezing (or repackaging) of it in formulas- kitsch, in short. (p. 19).

Berman then states that all of these factors are increasingly present on the American scene. The question is: how did America get itself into this presenting highly precarious situation in regard to the daily lives of its citizens?

## Future Societal Scenarios (Anderson)

In this adventure of civilization, Walter Truett Anderson, then— president of the American Division of the World Academy of Art and Science, postulates four different scenarios for the future of earthlings. In *The future of the self: Inventing the postmodern person* (1997), Anderson argues convincingly that current trends are adding up to an early 21st-century identity crisis for humankind. The creation of the present "modern self," he explains, began with Plato, Aristotle, and with the rights of humans in Roman legal codes.

Anderson argues that the developing conception of self bogged down in the Middle Ages, but fortunately was resurrected in the Renaissance Period of the second half of The Middle Ages. Since then the human "self " has been advancing like a "house afire" as the Western world has gone through an almost unbelievable transformation. Without resorting to historical detail, I will say only that scientists like Galileo and Copernicus influenced philosophers such as Descartes and Locke to foresee a world in which the self was invested with human rights.

"One World, Many Universes." Anderson's "One World, Many Universes" version is prophesied as the most likely to occur. This is a scenario characterized by (1) high economic growth, (2) steadily increasing technological progress, and (3) globalization combined with high psychological development. Such psychological maturity, he predicts, will be possible for a certain segment of the world's population because "active life spans will be gradually lengthened through various advances in health maintenance and medicine" (pp. 251-253). (This scenario may seem desirable, of course, to people who are coping reasonably well at present.)

However, it appears that a problem has developed at the beginning of this new century with this dream of individual achievement of inalienable rights and privileges. The modern self envisioned by Descartes—a rational, integrated self that Anderson likens to Captain Kirk at the command post of (the original Starship Enterprise—is having an identity crisis. The image of this bold leader (he or she!) taking us fearlessly into the great unknown has begun to fade as alternate scenarios for the future of life on Earth are envisioned.

For example, John Bogle of Vanguard, in his *The Battle for the Soul of Capitalism* (2007) argues that what he terms "global capitalism" is destroying the already uneasy balance between democracy as a political system and capitalism as an economic system. In a world where globalization and economic "progress" seemingly must be rejected because of catastrophic environmental concerns or "demands," the bold-future image could well "be replaced by a postmodern self; de-centered, multidimensional, and changeable" (p. 50).

Captain Kirk, or "George W," as he "boldly goes where no man has gone before"—this time to rid the world of terrorists)—is facing a second crucial change. As the American Government seeks to shape the world of the 21st century, based on Anderson's analysis, there is another force—the systemic-change force mentioned above—that is shaping the future. This all-powerful force may well exceed the Earth's ability to cope with what happens. As gratifying as such factors as "globalization along with economic growth" and "psychological development" may seem to the folks in Anderson's "One-World, Many Universes" scenario, there is a flip side to this prognosis. This image, Anderson identifies, as

"The Dysfunctional Family" scenario. It turns out that all of the "benefits" of so-called progress are highly expensive and available now only to relatively few of the six billion plus people on earth. Anderson foresees this scenario as "a world of modern people relatively happily doing their thing—modern people still obsessed with progress, economic gain, and organizational bigness—along with varieties of postmodern people being trampled and getting angry" [italics added] (p. 51). And, I might add further, as people get angrier, present-day terrorism in North America could seem like child's play.

## What Kind of A World Do You Want for Your Descendants?

What I am really asking here is whether you, the reader of these words, is cognizant of, and approves of, the situation as it is developing today. Are you (and I too!) simply "going along with the crowd" while taking the path of least resistance? Can we do anything to improve the situation by implementing an approach that could help to make the situation more beneficent and wholesome in perspective? What I am recommending is that the time is ripe for a country like Canada to distinguish itself more aggressively as being on a "different path" than the United States of America. To do this, however, individually and collectively, we would need to determine what sort of a world we (and our descendants) should be living in.

If you consider yourself an environmentalist, for example, the future undoubtedly looks bleak to you. What can we so to counter the strong business orientation of our society (i.e., being swept along with the "onward and upward" economic and technologic growth of American modernism)? Such is most certainly not the answer to all of our developing problems and issues. We should see ourselves increasingly as "New Agers" working to help Canada working to forge its own identity. I grant you, however, some sort of mass, non-religious "spiritual" transformation would have to take place for this to become a reality.

Let me offer one example based on my personal experience where I think Canada can make a good beginning in this respect. (Some who read this may wish to hang me in effigy [or literally!] for this assertion). Nevertheless I believe that Canada should strive to hold back the negative influences of America's approach to overly commercial, competitive sport in both universities and the public sector.

At present we are too often typically conforming blindly to a power structure in which sport is used largely by private enterprise for selfish purposes. The problem is this: opportunities for participation in all competitive sport—not just Olympic sport—moved historically from amateurism to semi-professionalism, and then on to full- blown professionalism.

The Olympic Movement, because of a variety of social pressures, followed suit in both ancient times and the present. When the International Olympic Committee gave that final push to the pendulum and openly admitted professional athletes to play in the Games, they may have pleased most of the spectators and all of the advertising and media representatives. But in so doing the floodgates were opened completely. The original ideals upon which the Games were reactivated were completely abandoned. This is what caused Sir Rees-Mogg in Britain, for example, to state that crass commercialism had won the day. This final abandonment of any semblance of what was the original Olympic ideal was the "straw that broke the camel's back." This ultimate decision regarding eligibility for participation has indeed been devastating to those people who earnestly believe that money and sport are like oil and water; they simply do not mix! Their response has been to abandon any further interest in, or support for, the entire Olympic Movement.

The question must, therefore be asked: "What should rampant professionalism in competitive sport at the Olympic Games mean to any given country out of the 200-plus nations involved?" This is not a simple question to answer responsibly. In this present brief statement, it should be made clear that the professed social values of a country should ultimately prevail—and that they will prevail in the final analysis. However, this ultimate determination will not take place overnight. The fundamental social values of a social system will eventually have a strong influence on the individual values held by most citizens in that country, also. If a country is moving toward the most important twin values of equalitarianism and achievement, for example, what implications does that have for competitive sport in that political entity under consideration? The following are some questions that should be asked before a strong continuing commitment is made to sponsor such involvement through governmental and/or private funding:

1. Can it be shown that involvement in competitive sport at one or the other of the three levels (i. e., amateur, semiprofessional, professional) brings about desirable social values (i. e., more value than disvalue)?

2. Can it be shown that involvement in competitive sport at one or the other of the three levels (i. e., amateur, semiprofessional, or professional) brings about desirable individual values of both an intrinsic and extrinsic nature (i. e., creates more value than disvalue)?

3. If the answer to Questions #1 and #2 immediately are both affirmative (i. e., that involvement in competitive sport at any or all of the three levels postulated [i. e., amateur, semiprofessional, and professional sport] provides a sufficient amount of social and individual value to warrant such promotion), can sufficient funds be made available to support or permit this promotion at any or all of the three levels listed?

4. If funding to supportparticipation in competitive sport at any or all of the three levels (amateur, semiprofessional, professional) is not available (or such participation is not deemed advisable), should priorities, as determined by the expressed will of the people, be established about the importance of each level to the country based on careful analysis of the potential social and individual values that may accrue to the society and its citizens from such competitive sport participation at oneor more levels? Further, as one aging person who encountered corruption and sleaze in the intercollegiate athletic structure of several major universities in the United States, I retreated to a Canadian university where the term "scholar-athlete" still implies roughly what it says. However, I now see problems developing on the Canadian inter-university sport scene as well. We have two choices before us. One choice is to do nothing about the "creeping semi-professionalism" that is occurring. This would require no great effort, of course. We can simply go along with the prevailing ethos of a North American society that is using sport to help in the promotion of social, as opposed to moral, character traits. In the process, "business as usual" will be supported one way or the other. A postmodern approach, conversely, would be one where specific geographic regions in Canada (the east, the far west.

Quebec, and the mid—west) reverse the trend toward semi-professionalism that is developing steadily. The pressures on university presidents and governing boards will increase steadily. Will they have wisdom and acumen to ward off this insidious possibility?

The reader can readily see where I am coming from with this discussion. I recommend strongly that we take a good look at what is implied when we challenge ourselves to consider what the deliberate creation of a postmodern world might do for an increasingly multiethnic Canada. Despite the return to a Conservative minority government, expanding the elements of postmodernism in Canada has a fighting chance to succeed. In the United States—forget it! Nevertheless, in its solid effort to become a unique, multicultural society, Canada may already be implementing what may be considered some of the better aspects of the concept of "postmodernism." For better or worse—and it may well be the latter—we are not so close to "the behemoth to the South" that we can't read the handwriting on the wall about what's happening "down there."

## How We Might Improve the Planet

Although the large majority of us wish that peace, happiness, harmony, and well-being could prevail globally, such has not happened. Prospects for such a happy state of affairs don't seem very likely in the foreseeable future either. Thus, to start with, I am inclined to wish forlornly that all of the clashing religious opinions and beliefs based on hoary tradition would silently go away. Then maybe prevailing world conditions would somehow begin to improve.

But this is wishful thinking unless improved institutions are created to take their place and make the entire world a better place in which to live. (Note here that I am recognizing the perennial designation of Canada—with all of its problems!—as one of the "best countries" in the world in which to live. Certainly I, for one, am not complaining—that's for certain!)

At this point I am anxious to convey the thought that it will only be through positive meliorism, philosophically speaking, that we humans will be able to do something to improve the prevailing disturbing, highly perplexing, and frustrating plight of the world as it struggles in the now (so tritely named) global village.

Implementing what is known as philosophical meliorism means simply that men and women working together in a spirit of brotherhood and sisterhood must work positively, not negatively, to make this "global ballgame" live up to the letter and spirit of the rules that are established by the U.N. and affiliated organizations. (As a former coach, I just had to throw in that 'sport speak' terminology.)

I believe that, in the absence of a sign from on high, we simply must—by ourselves (!)—dredge up the apocalypse (or unveiling) of the ethical core present in all world religions pointing to "a fuller understanding of the oneness of humankind." This we had better do very, very soon. In fact we need to do this by devising institutions that improve on these present outdated relics known as "time- proven" religions.

I say this because I am inclined to believe that the achievement for "good" of many of these theistic and/or spiritualistic approaches may soon be exceeded by their negative "bads" as their proponents parry and thrust repeatedly at their presumed arch-enemies and protagonists. (Speak to Mr. Rushdie and the many other religious and political outcasts around the world on this topic.)

So what I have to offer is not "yet another contemporary version of the now endlessly repeated moral counsels of despair," As I see it, positive meliorism (or working collectively to improve life) on the part of people of goodwill all over the world is the only way of salvation offered to us fallible humans in the absence of reasonable evidence that there is indeed a "Messianic vision" at the core of the 13 more or less established world religions.

How did I arrive at this position as my personal response to the persistent or perennial problems faced by humankind (i.e., war, famine, death, and pestilence)? As a young person, I soon realized the inherent limitations of a religious faith to which I was almost automatically bound by reason of birth. Instead of having some conception of theism of dubious historical origin foisted upon him or her in youth, my contention is that each young person should be encouraged by his or her parents to work this philosophic/religious problem out for himself or herself through careful reflection while growing to maturity. I believe that an individual's development and tentative "solution" about such matters would then have a deeper, more meaningful influence on the subsequent development of this individual as a socially oriented person, as well as a rational professional or tradesperson in an increasing complex and changing social environment.

Having personally been raised in a largely Judeo-Christian culture carried along by onrushing science and technology, I could not help but challenge what I perceived to be the inherent weaknesses of blind faith presented by fallible humans masking (literally) in the robes of this organized religion. In the process, what I thought I had learned from philosophers in my earlier days is also not being received with anywhere nearly the same authority as previously. Philosophers today, largely because of a truncated approach to their task, rarely speak to the larger questions of life and living.

So I soon came to accept a broader definition of religion, one conceived as "the pursuit of that which an educated and presumably enlightened person regards as most worthy and important in life." What I found to be most worthy was the advancement of knowledge for the betterment of humankind along with related teaching and professional service. This to me truly represented a personal challenge, and I reasoned that what I came up with should be fully worthy of a person's complete devotion.

Moreover, our culture has now become increasingly multiethnic and is resultantly characterized by the faiths and religious positions of all of these migrating peoples. I do respect the personal religious stances taken by many, but one soon comprehends that no one of the approximately 13 historical faiths has a corner on the market of religious truth. This situation has indeed created a highly confusing ethical "miasma," a situation where presently the thoughts of politicians, the writings of novelists, and the jibes of comedians seemed to be taking over on the subject of human values. Fortunately, however, there is a large amount of room for agreement among people of good will regardless of which faith or creed to which they subscribe. This would also be true for those who have never been involved, or are no longer involved, with some organized form of belief.

For example, I felt that we could agree that the cosmos as we know it is evolving or developing in time. It was obvious to me, also, that the mystery of this universe has already become a highly effective source of awe and reverence for many humans. Additionally, I could see as a developing young person that our growing knowledge of this vast cosmos was becoming increasingly valuable in helping us to guide our lives in an improved manner. Further, although some would debate this point, there is evidence of a type of progress through both inorganic and biological evolution.

Naively I had supposed that the world situation would improve markedly in my lifetime in the 20th century. Well, it has, and it hasn't. Fortunately, humankind is now beginning to realize that it has certain responsibilities, and accompanying powers, for the continuation of this evolution. We are gradually coming to an understanding that the practical application of universal brotherhood, undivided by nation, race, or creed, is vital if humankind wishes to survive. Whether we can progress as we hope to do in human affairs is a moot question.

The world is beginning to understand further that a form of democratic process in human relations provides the best opportunity for a person to develop to the maximum of his or her potentialities. Additionally, we are also steadily increasing worldwide awareness that the development of any one person shall not be at the expense of the group or society at large.

As defined above, I believe that philosophic/religious growth should be basic to all human life. It is an attitude of mind and "spirit" which should permeate all aspects of human endeavor. It is challenging to us that life as we know it in this universe appears to be characterized by creativity. Thus, it is reasonable to argue that the purpose of religion is to assist with the integration of all of a person's behavior with this presumed creativity within the universe. If religion is defined broadly, we may state that a critical and developing reason is a powerful aid in the search for a logically valid religious position.

I find that I want each individual to be free to seek philosophic-religious "truth" unhampered by official creed or outdated religious dogmas. Young people in schools and university should have an opportunity to study all of the world's great religions comparatively. In this way they will remain receptive to religious truth wherever it may be found.

I argue further that most—if not all!—aspects of life are (potentially) accessible to scientific study. This fact can be of enormous significance in the centuries that lie ahead. As the body of scientific knowledge grows, this will help to develop attitudes (as defined in psychology) that could lead to enlightened social action. Ultimately, to me this is a much truer criterion of the religious quality of a person's life than any religious ideas which are dutifully professed rote as part of a Sunday ritual.

As I see it, also, it is axiomatic that the church and the state should remain separate. Nevertheless, I do understand that it is most important for members of any religious group—acting as individuals—to take responsibility for positive social action. All enlightened citizens should be involved in the political process at some level.

This leads me finally to the conclusion that the hoary religious "truths" of the past are truly devoid of meaning for people facing the world of the 21st century. Some humanities scholars may believe, for example, that the "utopian speculation of the human imagination which constitutes the core of the liberal arts" is indeed a "moral counsel of despair" unless we all have "an encounter with a reality larger than the one we ourselves invent" (R. Woodman, The Univ. of Western Ontario). If Professor Woodman has had this "encounter," I am glad for him. However, I am finding that the Pennsylvania "Dutch" motto is creeping up on me fast. I am growing "too soon oldt und too late schmart." Thus, I am terribly worried about the future, an indeterminate period ahead about which we need to achieve a "Scotch Verdict."

## Can We Strengthen the Postmodern Influence?

My review of selected world, European, North American, regional, and local developments occurring in the final quarter of the 20th century may have created both positive and negative thoughts on your part. You might ask how this broadly based discussion relates to a plea for consideration of an increasingly postmodern social philosophy. My response to this question is "vigorous": "It doesn't" and yet

"It does." It doesn't relate or "compute" to the large majority of those functioning in the starkly modern "North American" world. The affirmative answer—that it does—is correct if we listen to the voices of those in the substantive minority who are becoming increasingly restless with the obvious negatives of the modernism that has spread so rapidly in the modern world.

To help reverse this disturbing development, some wise scholars have recommended that the discipline of philosophy should have some connection to the world as it was described above. Richard Rorty (1997), who was termed a so-called Neo-pragmatist, exhorted the presently "doomed liberal Left" in North America to join the fray again. The presumed shame of "the Left" should not be bolstered by a mistaken belief that only those who agree with the Marxist position that capitalism must be eradicated are "true Lefts." Rorty recommends that philosophy once again become characterized as a "search for wisdom," a search that seeks conscientiously to answer the many pressing issues and problems looming before humankind worldwide.

While most philosophers were "elsewhere engaged," some within the fold considered what has been called postmodernism carefully. For example, in *Crossing the Postmodern Divide* by Albert Borgmann (Chicago: The University of Chicago Press, 1992), it was refreshing to find such a clear assessment of the present situation. Time and again in discussions about postmodernism, I have encountered what I soon began to characterize as gobbledygook (i.e., planned obfuscation?). This effort by Borgmann was solid, down-to-earth, and comprehensible. However, in the final two pages, he veered to a Roman-Catholic position that that he calls postmodern realism as the answer to the plight caused by modernism. It is his right, of course, to state his personal opinion after describing the current political and social situation so accurately. However, if he could have brought himself to it, or if he had thought it possible, it might have been better if he had spelled out several alternative directions for humankind to go in the 21st century. (Maybe we should be thankful that he thought any one might be able to save it!)

With his argument that "postmodernism must become, for better or worse, something other than modernism," Borgmann explains that:

[postmodernism] already exhibits two distinct tendencies: The first is to refine technology. Here postmodernism shares with modernists an unreserved allegiance to technology, but it differs from modernism in giving technology a hyper-fine and hyper-complex design. This ten- dency I call hyper-modernism. The alternative tendency is to outgrow technology as a way of life and to put it to the service of reality, of the things that command our respect and grace our life. This I call postmodern realism (p. 82).

At what point could we argue that the modern epoch or era has come to an end and that civilization is ready to put hyper-modernism aside and embrace Borgmann's postmodern realism—or any form of postmodernism for that matter? Can we hope to find agreement that this epoch is approaching closure because a substantive minority of the populace is challenging many of the fundamental beliefs of modernism? The "substantive minority" may not be large enough yet, but the reader may be ready to agree that indeed the world is moving into a new epoch as the proponents of postmodernism have been affirming over recent decades. Within such a milieu all professions would probably find great difficulty crossing this so-called, postmodern gap (chasm, divide, whatever you may wish to call it). Scholars argue convincingly that many in democracies, under girded by the various rights being propounded (e.g., individual freedom, privacy), have not yet come to believe that they have found a supportive "liberal consensus" within their respective societies.

My contention is that "post-modernists"—whether they recognize themselves as belonging to this group—now form a substantive minority that supports a more humanistic, pragmatic, liberal consensus in society. Yet they recognize that present- day society is going to have difficulty crossing any such postmodern divide. Many traditionalists in democratically oriented political systems may not like everything they see in front of them today, but as they look elsewhere they flinch even more. After reviewing where society has been, and where it is now, two more questions need to be answered. Where is society heading, and—most importantly—where should it be heading?

As despairing as one might be of society's direction today, the phenomenon of postmodernism—with its accompanying deconstructionist analytic technique affirming the idea that the universe is valueless with no absolute—brings one up short quickly. Take your choice: bleak pessimism or blind optimism. The former seems to be more dangerous to humankind's future that that of an idealistic future "under the sheltering arms of a Divine Father." Yet, some argue that Nietzsche's philosophy of being, knowledge, and morality supports the basic dichotomy espoused by the philosophy of being in the post-modernistic position. I can understand at once, therefore, why it meets with opposition by those whose thought has been supported by traditional theocentrism.

A better approach, I recommend, might be one of "positive meliorism" in which humankind is exhorted to "take it from here and do its best to improve the world situation." In the process we should necessarily inquire: "What happened to the "Enlightenment ideal"? This was supposed to be America's chief criterion of progress, but it has gradually but steadily undergone such a decisive change since the founding of the Republic. That change is at once a cause and a reflection of our current disenchantment with technology.

Post-modernists do indeed subscribe to a humanistic, anthropocentric belief as opposed to the traditional theocentric position. They would probably subscribe, therefore to what Berelson and Steiner in the mid-1960s postulated as a behavioral science image of man and woman. This view characterized the human as a creature continuously adapting reality to his or her own ends. Such thought undoubtedly challenges the authority of theological positions, dogmas, ideologies, and some scientific "infallibles".

A moderate post-modernist—holding a position I feel able to subscribe to once I am able to bring it all into focus—would at least listen to what the "authority" had written or said before criticizing or rejecting it. A fully committed post-modernist goes his or her own way by early, almost automatic, rejection of all tradition. Then this person presumably relies simply on a personal interpretation and subsequent diagnosis to muster the authority to challenge any or all icons or "lesser gods" extant in society.

Of course, the world must move into the future strongly and boldly, but it will also have to proceed with great care and concern. This is why I think we need to achieve a "Scotch Verdict" about the future. "Getting in league with the future" or "future forecasting" can be carried out best by making a sincere, solid effort to understand what futuristics or futurology is all about. One could take the next step and apply these findings to one or more aspects of our lives. In Visions of the Future, a publication of the well-known Hudson Institute, we are urged to tailor our thinking to three ways of looking at the future: (1) the possible future, (2) the probable future, and (3) the preferable future.

As you might imagine, the possible future includes everything that could happen, and thus perceptions of the future must be formed by us individually and collectively. The probable future refers to occurrences that are likely to happen, and so here the range of alternatives must be considered. Finally, the preferable future relates to an approach whereby people make choices, thereby indicating how they would like things to happen. Underlying all of this are certain basic assumptions or premises such as

(1) that the future hasn't been predetermined by some force or power; (2) that the future cannot be accurately predicted because we don't understand the process of change that fully; and

(3) that the future will undoubtedly be influenced by choices that people make, but won't necessarily turn out the way they want it to be (Amara, 1981).

As we all appreciate, people have been predicting the future for thousands of years, undoubtedly with a limited degree of success. Considerable headway has been made, of course, since the time when animal entrails were examined to provide insight about the future (one of the techniques of so-called divination). Nowadays, for example, methods of prediction include forecasting by the use of trends and statistics.

John Naisbitt and The Naisbitt Group stated in the first *Megatrends* volume (1982): "the most reliable way to anticipate the future is by understanding the present." Hence they monitor occurrences all over the world through a technique of descriptive method known as content analysis. They actually monitor the amount of space given to various topics in newspapers—an approach they feel is valid because "the news-reporting process is forced choice in a closed system."

Melnick and associates, in Visions of the Future, discuss another aspect of futuristics: the question of "levels of certainty." They explain that the late Herman Kahn, an expert in this area, often used the term "Scotch Verdict" when he was concerned about the level of certainty available prior to making a decision. This idea was borrowed from the Scottish system of justice in which a person charged with the commission of a crime can be found "guilty," "not guilty," or "not been proven guilty." This "not been proven guilty" (or "Scotch") verdict implies there is probably enough evidence to demonstrate that the person charged could be guilty, but that insufficient evidence has been presented to end all reasonable doubt about the matter.

With this continuum that has been developed, at one end we can state we are 100% sure that such-and-such is not true. Accordingly, at the other end of the continuum we can state we are 100% sure that such-and-such is the case. Obviously, in-between these two extremes are gradations of the level of certainty. From here this idea has been carried over to the realm of future forecasting.

There is good reason to believe that we are not considering sufficiently the "Great Transition" that humankind has been experiencing, how there has been a pre-industrial stage, an industrial stage and, finally, a postindustrial stage that has evidently arrived in North America first. Each of the stages has its characteristics that must be recognized. For example, in pre-industrial society there was slow population growth, people lived simply with very little money, and the forces of nature made life very difficult. When the industrial stage or so-called modernization entered the picture, population growth was rapid, wealth increased enormously, and people became increasingly less vulnerable to the destructive forces of nature.

The assumption in so-called modern society is that comprehension of the transition that is occurring can give us some insight as to what the future might hold—not that we can be "100% sure," but at least we might be able to achieve a "Scotch Verdict." If North America is that part of the world that is the most economically and technologically advanced, and as a result completed the Great Transition by becoming a postindustrial culture first, we must be aware of what this will mean to our society. Thus, some argue that we have probably already entered a "super-industrial period" of the Industrial Stage in which "projects will be very large scale; services will be readily available, efficient and sophisticated; people will have vastly increased leisure time; and many new technologies will be created."

It is important that we understand what is happening as we move further forward into what presumably is the final or third stage of the Great Transition. It should be made clear that the level of certainty here in regard to predictions is at Kahn's "Scotch Verdict" point on the continuum. The world has never faced this situation before; so, we don't know exactly how to date the beginning of such a stage. Nevertheless, it seems to be taking place right now with the super-industrial period having started after World War II. As predicted, those developments mentioned above (e.g., services readily available) appear to be continuing.

Some postulate that the rate of population growth is slower than it was 20 years ago; yet, it is also true that people are living longer. Next it is estimated that a greater interdependence among nations and the steady development of new technologies will contribute to a steadily improving economic climate for underdeveloped nations. Finally, it is forecast that advances in science and accompanying technology will bring almost innumerable technologies to the fore that will affect life styles immeasurably all over the world.

This discussion could continue indefinitely, but the important points to be made here are emerging rapidly. First, we need a different way of looking at the subject of so-called natural resources. In this interdependent world, this "global village" if you will, natural resources are more than just the sum of raw materials. They include also the application of technology, the organizational bureaucracy to cope with the materials, and the resultant usefulness of the resource that creates supply and demand. The point seems to be that the total resource picture (as explained here) is reasonably optimistic if correct decisions are made about raw materials, energy, food production, and use of the environment. These are admittedly rather large "IFS".

Finally in "forecasting the future," the need to understand global problems of two types should be stressed. One group is called "mostly understandable problems," and they are solvable. Here reference is made to:

(1) population growth,

(2) natural resource issues,

(3) acceptable environmental health,

(4) shift in society's economic base to service occupations, and

(5) effect of advanced technology.

However, it is the second group classified as "mostly uncertain problems," and these are the problems that could bring on disaster.

First, the Great Transition is affecting the entire world, and the eventual outcome of this new type of cultural change is uncertain. Thus we must be ready for these developments attitudinally.

Second, in this period of changing values and attitudes, people in the various countries and cultures have much to learn, and they will have to make great adjustments as well.

Third, there is the danger that society will—possibly unwittingly—stumble into some irreversible environmental catastrophe (e.g., upper-atmosphere ozone depletion).

Fourth, the whole problem of weapons, wars, and terrorism, and whether the world will be able to stave off all-out nuclear warfare, and

Fifth, and finally, whether bad luck and bad management will somehow block the entire world from undergoing the Great Transition successfully—obviously a great argument for the development of management art and science.

# Epilogue

In the Epilogue I have included a variety of brief articles I have written recently. I have chosen this aspect of society and education to make clear what happened and what is continuing to happen both to sport in society and to physical activity education within education. I believe they lay bare what to me then and now explains what "had been done" to competitive sport *in* society and *by* society. And, further, what *"hasn't happened!"* to the large major it children and youth who "show the results" (e.g., obesity and lack of fitness!)! I believe that America has "led the way" in the Western world in this regard. Other countries, including Canada to a lesser degree except for the sport of hockey, are gradually but surely following in America's footsteps.

It seems obvious to me that sport is bound to reflect society—not the opposite! The sporting activity of my youth that continued up through my college years was amateur to the nth degree. I enjoyed it tremendously because it enhanced and enriched my life in a variety of ways. Hence, when I got a chance to work in profession of education as a physical educator/coach, there was an automatic connection or relationship with a previous quite good sport and related activity experience as well. However, I did see deficiencies in "various directions". This had a great deal to do with convincing me that entering the field of physical activity education was a good choice for my life work.

Subsequently this profession "grew on me" as I actually did work become most enthusiastic after leaving YMCA work and then with my employment at Yale University in the 1940s and Western University in Ontario in the 1950s. For example, both of these institutions sponsored "solid" physical education programs for all students, as well as athletic teams for athletes who were bona fide students academically. These athletes received financial help only when there was proven financial need.

However, as I moved to work at state universities such as The University of Michigan and the University of Illinois, the quality of the experience changed gradually. Football first, and then basketball somewhat later, have grown to "enormous heights" in relation to other sports in the athletic program. In the process they have become pawns serving several of the universities' fundamental needs for survival in an increasingly commercialized environment. It is a national disgrace what this development has done to the "educational soul" of Division I and Division II university athletic programs within the National Collegiate Athletic Association!

Additionally, and most importantly as I have sought most diligently to emphasize, the physical activity and related health education program (including intramural athletics) has been severely neglected and/or disregarded over the years of the twentieth century on into the early years of the twenty-first century. The accuracy of this assessment has been made abundantly clear in The *2012 Shape of the Nation Report: Status of Physical Education* in America provided by National Association for Sport and Physical Education (AAHPERD) and the American Heart Association. Although of the 50 states and the District of Columbia, 38 states do require physical education programs in the schools, the majority of them vitiate the effectiveness of these established regulations by permitting all sorts of waivers and exemptions.

## Developmental Physical Activity Should Create Positive Values

Despite this steady increase in competitive sport offerings either within education or in the public sector, just about all of us would admit readily that there should always be more to life than sport. We are quick to criticize the young person who doesn't appear to be rounding into normal maturity. At a certain age we typically expect youth to become interested in the opposite sex—an unrealistic expectation for all today—and develop heterosexual social recreational interests.

We like to think also that young people are developing in other areas of recreational interest—in communicative interests such as conversation and discussion, as well as in writing and in learning interests that indicate a desire to know more about many aspects of the world that interest them. This development should further extend to creative and aesthetic interests where the opportunity is afforded to create beauty according to individual appreciation of what constitutes artistic expression of form, color, sound, or movement.

However, I agree that we can't state absolutely or precisely that such-and-such a program *should* be followed. Living one's life will always be (we hope) an art rather than a science. Nevertheless, people who are maturing should proceed basically on the best available theory based on scientific findings. The opinions of educators, of medical scientists, and of social scientists point in a similar direction, of course, but often this is still based on inadequate evidence.

*Nevertheless, I believe strongly that physical activity education (including athletics and related health instruction), broadly interpreted and experienced under wise educational or recreational conditions, can serve humankind as a worthwhile social institution contributing vitally to the well being, ongoing health, and longevity of humankind.*

## This Disoriented Field Involving Human Physical Activity Should Have a Mission?

Despite my italicized statement immediately above, this message is simply not getting across to the population in advanced countries to such an extent that it is being implemented to the right degree! Every year the *Quest journal* devotes one issue to report the proceedings of the previous year's annual meeting of the American Academy of Kinesiology and Physical Education. The 2006 theme of the AAKPE was "Kinesiology: ***Defining the Academic Core of Our Discipline."***

Michael Wade, director the School of Kinesiology at the University of Minnesota, was asked to be the conference summarizer. His "Quo Vadis Kinesiology?" analysis raised some excellent, pointed questions about the essence of the program held. Accepting the fact that the field ("we" referring to members of the Academy "have at least tentatively decided to call itself kinesiology," Wade continued with a number of insightful reactions that pointed out our field's highly disturbing lack of orientation that is characterized by the absence of a clear statement of mission.

*(Note: Wade, M. (2007) "Quo Vadis Kinesiology?" In Quest, 59, 1, pp. 170-173.)*

I immediately wrote him expressing some of the thoughts below. For example, it seemed that we had some agreement as to the "rudderlessness" of the Academy and the entire field itself. As I read the proceedings, I was greatly discouraged by the program planning and subsequent proceedings of this disparate group. The individual statements of the invited speakers at this meeting were generally excellent. However, it was the central focus that was so woefully inadequate!

These men and women are the self-proclaimed 100 "top, active scholars and scientists" of "kinesiology and physical education" in the USA! This is the scholarly group that deliberately separated itself in the early 1990s from the founding professional society, the one that spawned us all! (The AAHPERD was originally the Association for the Advancement of Physical Education in 1885).

*Note: At this point I should explain my intense interest in the topic] because I was inducted as a Fellow in the [then] Academy of Physical Education in 1966 and subsequently was elected president. Finally, I received its highest recognition: the Hetherington Award.)*

Now, well into my 70th active year in the field that has been searching for a "consensual name" for more than a century, I admit that I too thought that the question had been resolved. I can remember C. H. McCloy (arguably the top "physical educator/scientist" of the first half of the 20th century) saying: "To change the name away from *physical education* now would be akin to rolling back Niagara Falls." (Interestingly, this interesting predictions seem to has on occasion been accomplished.

I am trying hard, also, not to become "un ancien". (Since the turn of the 21$^{st}$ century, some 21 books, other monographs, and 21 articles of mine have been published.) The AAKPE's "progress" or "status"—admittedly of long standing and significant stature in this field—is in a way something like that of the more recent International Association for Sport Philosophy, another group of which I was president also in an "earlier life." The public doesn't know that the IAPS exists; the field of education doesn't know it exists; and physical activity educators and coaches worldwide don't know (or care!) that it's there either. Interestingly, the people from different "specialties" within each of these societies don't typically "speak" to each other during the year as well. Hence, I must ask: Whom have I missed that members of both societies are not speaking to?

My question is simply this: If these groups do not relate strongly to the public, to education, and to the established field of practitioners closest to the discipline they represent, what good are they? (Oh yes, for the moment I forgot. Their societal publications are vital for individuals' on-the-job promotion and for obtaining funds to attend conferences!) In semi-retirement at age 93, I will continue—for a while, I hope—to write for those in the field concerned about "physical activity education in exercise, sport, dance, and physical recreation—accompanied by related health education—for normal, accelerated, special people of all ages ".

As members of a quasi-discipline, quasi-profession, we want this for everybody. In addition, we can get knowledge and assistance for the fulfillment of our mission by turning to all of the humanities, the social science, and the natural sciences—as well as a variety of professions and working specifically with them. For example, I ask, what knowledge is "out there" in the subject of geography that can further healthful physical activity? Or in anthropology? Or kinanthropometry?

Fundamentally, as I said in an e-book: "As professionals we don't know what we don't know because the burgeoning knowledge component of our various sub disciplinary and sub-professional components has gotten away from any one person!" Frankly, this is where our professional associations worldwide can and should be helping practitioners by providing "evolving ordered generalizations" of scientific and scholarly findings about developmental physical activity.

Frankly, and bluntly, I can come to no other conclusion other than that a solid segment of the people in our field at the university level are undoubtedly candidates for recognition as the most disoriented group of scientists and scholars in existence. I'm sure there are other disoriented groups "out there" as well that I'm not aware of. These are people who have what the late Paul Hunsicker of our field (Michigan, Ann Arbor) used to call "tunnel vision."

We in this field *within education* have not been given the necessary support to work at all levels within the field of education (children, teens, adults, etc.) In addition, the field was not able to flourish or develop in society at large to work with adults, "middle-agers," and seniors. ***YET THE DIRE NEED FOR REGULAR PLANNED PHYSICAL ACTIVITY (Exercise!) FOR ALL THROUGHOUT THEIR LIVES IS SO OBVIOUS!***

What did happen? It has now become a little bit like what Jimmy Durante, the late comedian, used to say: "Everybody's trying to get into the act!" A cacophony of "other voices" has entered the picture to fill the vacuum! Even my *Mayo Clinic Health Letters* includes sound physical activity education procedures written by presumably unqualified medical person because there is no author attribution)! Interestingly, there isn't a week that goes by without some new study pointing out that regular physical activity can cure or improve "this or that" in people's lives or lengthen their lives.

In addition, I am forced to ask further: What is going on here? How many of these graduates in the discipline of kinesiology (i.e., the study of movement literally) will be helping people in society to live better lives based on their qualifications as "movement analysts"? I'm certain that some will, but who knows about it? Where is the proof that these graduates of kinesiology programs are helping people of all ages to analyze movement kinematically (much less understand such movement **KINETICALLY**)? Shouldn't that—by definition!—be their function based on this Greek nomenclature?

Further, I would like to see the rationalization for the positions these graduates are engaged in. Where are they? What are they doing? Do we really know? A small percentage does go to the units of professional education on campuses to become teachers in a system where their efforts will continue to be downgraded. Why downgraded? Because **WE** in the field evidently haven't "made our case" strongly enough. Any statement of the field of physical activity education's mission should proclaim our hope that all people **WORLDWIDE,** people of all ages and conditions actively will be involved with satisfaction in healthful and joyful physical activity.

# Based on Established Principles, We Should Guarantee the Best Type of Developmental Physical Activity to Youth

## Physical Activity Education's Fourteen (14) "Principal Principles"

Principle 1:    The "Reversibility Principle". The first principle affirms that cardiovascular conditioning is inherently reversible in the human body;

Principle 2:    The "Overload Principle". The second principle states that a muscle or muscle group must be taxed beyond that to which it is accustomed, or it won't develop;

Principle 3:    The "Flexibility Principle". This principle indicates that a human must put the body's various joints through the range of motion for which they are intended. Inactive joints become increasingly inflexible until immobility sets in;

Principle 4:    The "Bone Density Principle". This principle asserts that developmental physical activity throughout life helps significantly to maintain the density of a human's bones;

Principle 5:    The "Gravity Principle". This principle explains that maintaining muscle-group strength throughout life, while standing or sitting, helps the human fight against the force of gravity that is working continually to break down the body's structure;

Principle 6:  The "Relaxation Principle". Principle 6 states that the skill of relaxation is one that people must acquire in today's increasingly complex world;

Principle 7:  The "Aesthetic Principle". This principle explains that a person has either an innate or culturally determined need to "look good" to himself/herself and to others;

Principle 8:  The "Integration Principle". Principle 8 demonstrates that developmental physical activity is an important means whereby the individual can "fully involved" as a living organism. By their very nature, physical activities in exercise, sport, play, and expressive movement demand full attention from the organism—often in the face of opposition—and therefore involve complete psycho-physical integration;

Principle 9:  The "Integrity Principle". The principle of integrity implies that a completely integrated psycho-physical activity should correspond **ETHICALLY** with the avowed ideals and standards of society. (Thus, the "integrity principle" goes hand in hand with desirable integration of the human's various aspects [so-called unity of body and mind in the organism explained in Principle 8 immediately above]};

Principle 10:  The "Priority of the Person Principle". Principle 10 affirms that any physical activity in sport, play, and exercise sponsored through public or private agencies should be conducted in such a way that the welfare of the individual comes first (i.e., sport must serve as a "social servant");

Principle 11:  The "Live Life to Its Fullest Principle". This principle explains that, viewed in one sense, human movement is what distinguishes the individual from the rock on the ground. Unless the body is moved with reasonable vigor according to principles 1-6 above, it will not serve a person best throughout life;

Principle 12:     The "Fun and Pleasure Principle". Principle 12 states that the human is normally a "seeker of fun and pleasure," and that a great deal of the opportunity for such enjoyment can be derived from full, active bodily movement; and

Principle 13:     The "Longevity Principle". This recently conceived principle affirms the possibility that regular developmental physical activity throughout life can help a person live longer (Zeigler, 1994).

Principle 14:     The "Physical Fitness & Learning—Correlation Principle" affirms that evidence accumulating is showing a positive relationship between physical fitness and what is termed as academic achievement.

## The Professional Task Ahead

What, then, is the professional task ahead? First, we should truly understand why we have chosen this profession as we rededicate ourselves anew to the study and dissemination of knowledge, competencies, and skills in developmental physical activity in sport, exercise, and related expressive movement. Concurrently, of course, we need to determine exactly what it is that we are professing.

Second, as either professional practitioners or instructors involved in professional preparation, we should search for young people of high quality in all the attributes needed for success in the field. Then we should follow through to help them develop lifelong commitments so that our profession can achieve its democratically agreed-upon goals. We should also prepare young people to serve in the many alternative careers in sport, exercise, dance, and recreational play that are becoming increasingly available in our society.

Third, we must place *quality* as the first priority of our professional endeavors. Our personal involvement and specialization should include a high level of competency and skill under girded by solid knowledge about the profession. It can be argued that our professional task is as important as any in society. Thus, the present is no time for indecision, half-hearted commitment, imprecise knowledge, and general unwillingness to stand up and be counted in debate with colleagues within our field and in allied professions and related disciplines, not to mention the public.

Fourth, the obligation is ours. If we hope to reach our potential, we must sharpen our focus and improve the quality of our professional effort. Only in this way will we be able to guide the modification process that the profession is currently undergoing toward the achievement of our highest professional goals. This is the time, right now, to employ exercise, sport, dance, and play to make our reality more healthful, more pleasant, more vital, and more life enriching. By "living fully in one's body," behavioral science men and women will be adapting and shaping this phase of reality to their own ends.

Finally, such improvement will not come easily; it can only come through the efforts of professional people making quality decisions, through the motivation of people to change their sedentary lifestyles, and through our professional assistance in guiding people as they strive to fulfill such motivation in their movement patterns. Our missions in the years ahead is to place this special quality in all of our professional endeavor.

## What Should The Field of Developmental Physical Activity Do in the 21st Century?

What should the field of developmental physical activity do—perhaps what *must* we do—to ensure that it will move more decisively and rapidly in the direction of what might be called status *within* education and recognized status as a profession in society at large? Granting that the various social forces will impact upon us, what can we do collectively in the years immediately ahead? These positive steps should be actions that will effect a workable consolidation of purposeful accomplishments on the part of those men and women who have a concern for the future of developmental physical activity as a valuable component of human life from birth to death. The following represent a number of categories joined with action principles that are related insofar as possible to the "modifications" that have been taking place in our field. We should seek a North American consensus on the steps spelled out below. Then we, as dedicated professional educators, should take as rapid and strong action as we can muster through our professional associations in America and Canada. These recommended steps are as follows:

*A Sharper Image.* Because in the past the field of physical education has tried to be "all things to all people," and presently doesn't know exactly what it does stand for, we should now sharpen our image and improve the quality of our efforts by focusing primarily on developmental physical activity—specifically, human motor performance in sport, exercise, and related expressive movement. As we sharpen our image, we should make a strong effort to cooperate with those who are working in the private agency and commercial sectors by helping them to get organized under a *single* national association with related state and/or provincial entities. This implies further that we will extend our efforts to promote the finest type of developmental physical activity for people of all ages whether they be members of what are considered to be "normal, accelerated, or special" populations.

*Our Field's Name.* Because all sorts of name changes have been implemented (a) to explain either what people think we are doing or should be doing, or (b) to camouflage the presumed "unsavory" connotation of the term "physical education" that evidently conjures up the notion of a "dumb jock" working with the lesser part of a tri-partite human body, we should continue to focus primarily on *developmental physical activity* as defined immediately above while moving toward an acceptable working term for our profession. In so doing, we should keep in mind the field's bifurcated nature in that it has both theoretical and practical (or disciplinary and professional) aspects. At the moment we are called sport and physical education or physical activity and recreation (NASPE or AAPAR, respectively) within the Alliance (AAHPERD) professionally and physical and health education in a significant number of elementary and secondary schools in Canada (PHE Canada). A desirable name for our under girding discipline would be *developmental physical activity*, and we could delineate this by our inclusion of exercise, sport, and expressive movement. (As this book is being written, the terms "kinesiology" and "human kinetics" (from the Greek word *kinesis* are looming ever larger in both the United States and Canada as a name for the undergraduate degree program in our field. However, it is most difficult to see this word catching on in the public schools.)

*A Tenable Body of Knowledge.* Inasmuch as various social forces and professional concerns have placed us in a position where we don't know where or what our body of knowledge is, we will strongly support the idea of disciplinary definition and the continuing development of *a body of knowledge* based on such a consensual definition. From this must come a merging of tenable scientific theory in keeping with societal values and computer technology so that we will gradually, steadily, and increasingly provide our members with the knowledge that they need to perform as top-flight professionals. As professionals we simply must possess the requisite knowledge, competencies, and skills necessary to provide developmental physical activity services of a high quality to the public both within education and also in society at large.

*Our Own Professional Association.* Inasmuch as there is insufficient support of our own professional association for a variety of reasons, we need to develop voluntary and mandatory mechanisms that relate membership in **one** *professional* organization both directly and indirectly to stature within the field. We simply must now commit ourselves to work tirelessly and continually to promote the welfare of professional practitioners who are serving the public in the educational system and also in the larger society. Incidentally, it may be necessary to exert any available pressures to encourage people to give first priority to our own scholarly and professional groups (as opposed to those of related disciplines and/or allied professions). The logic behind this dictum is that our own survival comes first for us!

*Professional Licensing.* Although most teachers/coaches in the schools, colleges, and universities are seemingly protected indefinitely by the shelter of the all-embracing teaching profession, we should now move rapidly and strongly to seek official recognition of our endeavors in public, semi-public, and private agency work and in commercial organizations relating to developmental physical activity *through professional licensing at the state or provincial level.* Further, we should encourage individuals to apply for voluntary registration as qualified practitioners at the federal level in both the United States and Canada.

*Harmony Within The Field.* Because an unacceptable series of gaps and misunderstandings has developed among those in our field concerned primarily with the bio-scientific aspects of human motor performance, those concerned with the social-science and humanities aspects, those concerned with the general education of all students, those concerned with the professional preparation of physical activity educators/coaches, and those connected with the professional preparation of sport managers—all at the college or university level—we will strive to work for *a greater balance and improved understanding* among these essential entities within the profession.

*Harmony Among The Allied "Professions".* Keeping in mind that the original field of physical education has spawned a number of allied "professions" down through the years of the 20th century, *we should strive to comprehend what they claim that they do professionally, and where there may be a possible overlap with what we claim that we do.* Where disagreements prevail, they should be ironed out to the greatest extent possible at the national level within the Alliance (AAHPERD) in the United States and within Physical & Health Education Canada (PHE Canada).

*The Relationship With Intercollegiate Athletics/Sport.* An ever-larger wedge has been driven between units of physical education and interscholastic and intercollegiate athletics in educational institutions where gate receipts are a strong and basic factor. Such a rift serves no good purpose and is counter to the best interests of both groups. *Developmental physical activity available through the services of physical activity educators should remain separate from varsity sport in those universities where the promotion of highly organized, often commercialized athletics exists (e.g., NCAA Division I and II institutions).. However, we must work for greater understanding and harmony with those people who are primarily interested in this enterprise.* At the same time it is imperative that we do all in our power to maintain athletics in a sound educational perspective within our schools, colleges, and universities.

*The Relationship with Intramurals and Recreational Sports.* Intramurals and recreational sports is in a transitional state at present in that it has proved that it is "here to stay" at the college and university level. Nevertheless, intramurals hasn't really taken hold yet, generally speaking, as a program of after-school sport experiences at the high school level, despite the fact that it has a great deal to offer the large majority of "normal" and "special-needs" students in what may truly be called *educational* sport. Everything considered, I believe (1) that— both philosophically and practically—intramurals and recreational sports ought to remain within the sphere of the physical activity education field; (2) that it is impractical and inadvisable to attempt to subsume all non-curricular activities on campus under one department or division; and (3) that departments and divisions of physical activity education ought to work for consensus on the idea that *intramurals and recreational sports are co-curricular in nature* and deserve regular funding as laboratory experience in the same manner that general education course experiences in physical activity education receives its funding for instructional purposes.

*Guaranteeing Equal Opportunity.* Because "life, liberty, and the pursuit of happiness" are guaranteed to all in North American society. as a profession we should move positively and strongly to see to it that *equal opportunity* is indeed provided to the greatest possible extent to women, to minority groups, and to special populations (e.g., the handicapped) as they seek to improve the quality of their lives through the finest type of experience in the many activities of our field.

*Holding High the Physical Activity Education (including Sport) Identity.* In addition to the development of the allied professions (e.g., school health education) in the second quarter of the twentieth century, we witnessed the advent of a disciplinary thrust in the 1960s that was followed by a splintering of many of the various "knowledge components" and subsequent formation of many different societies. These developments have undoubtedly weakened the field of (sport and) physical education as it is now called within the NASPE and physical activity and recreation within the AAPAR. Thus, it is now more important than ever that we *hold high the physical activity education identity* as we continue to promote vigorously the scholarly academies that have been formed within the AAHPERD (and the similar scholarly interest groups [SIGS] with PHE Canada). Additionally we should re-affirm and delineate even more carefully our relationship with our allied professions.

*Applying a Competency Approach.* Whereas the failures and inconsistencies of the established educational process have become increasingly apparent, *we will as a field within the education profession and a profession in society at large explore the educational possibilities of a competency approach* as it might apply to general education, to professional preparation, and to all aspects of our professional endeavor in public, semi-public, private, and commercial agency endeavors *Managing the Enterprise.* All professionals in the unique field of physical activity education (including sport) are managers—but to varying degrees. The "one course in administration" approach with no laboratory or internship experience of earlier times is simply not sufficient for the future. There is an urgent need to apply a competency approach in the preparation (as well as in the continuing education) of those who will serve as managers either within educational circles or elsewhere in the society at large.

*Ethics and Morality in Physical Activity Education (and Educational/Recreational Sport).* In the course of the development of the best professions, the various, embryonic professional groups have gradually become conscious of the need for a set of professional ethics—that is, a set of professional *obligations* that are established as *norms* for practitioners in good standing to follow. Our profession needs both a creed and a detailed code of ethics right now as we move ahead in our development. Such a move is important because, generally speaking, ethical confusion prevails in North American society. Development of a sound code of ethics, combined with steady improvement in the three essentials of a fine profession (i.e., an extensive period of training, a significant intellectual component that must be mastered before the profession is practiced, and a recognition by society that the trained person can provide a basic, important service to its citizens) would relatively soon place us in a much firmer position to claim that we are indeed members of a fine profession. (Zeigler, 2007).

*Reunifying the Field's Integral Elements.* Because there now appears to be reasonable agreement that what is now called the field of sport and physical education (within NASPE) and physical activity and recreation (within AAPAR), *we will is concerned primarily with developmental physical activity as manifested in human motor performance in sport, exercise, and related expressive movement. In addition, we will now work for the reunification of those elements of our profession that should be uniquely ours within our disciplinary definition of developmental physical activity.*

*Cross-Cultural Comparison and International Understanding.* We have done reasonably well in the area of international relations within the Western world due to the solid efforts of many dedicated people over a considerable period of time, but at present we need to redouble our efforts to make cross-cultural comparisons of physical activity education (including educational/recreational sport) while reaching out for international understanding and cooperation in both the Western and Eastern blocs. Much greater understanding on the part of all of the concepts of 'communication,' 'diversity,' and 'cooperation' is required for the creation of a better life for all in a *peaceful* world. Our profession can contribute significantly toward this long—range objective.

*Permanency and Change.* Inasmuch as the "principal principles" espoused for physical education in the early 1950s by the late Arthur Steinhaus of George Williams College have now been extended from four to fourteen, all still apply most aptly to our professional endeavors, *we will continue to emphasize that which is timeless in our work, while at the same time accepting the inevitability of certain societal change.*

*Improving the Quality and Length of Life.* Since our field is **unique** within education and in society, and since fine living and professional success involve so much more than the important verbal and mathematical skills, we will emphasize strongly that education is a lifelong enterprise. Further, we will stress that *the quality and* *length of life can be improved significantly through the achievement of an acceptable degree of kinetic awareness and through heightened experiences in exercise, sport, and related expressive movement.*

*Reasserting Our "Will to Win".* Although the developments of the past 30 years have undoubtedly created an uneasiness within the profession, and have raised doubts on the part of some as to our possession of a "will to win" through the achievement of the highest type of professional status, *we pledge ourselves to make still greater efforts to become vibrant and stirring through absolute dedication and commitment in our professional endeavors.* Ours is a high calling as we seek to improve the quality of life for all through the finest type of developmental physical activity in sport, exercise, and related expressive movement.

# Babe Ruth or Lou Gehrig:
# An American Dilemma

"There is an appalling shortage of genuine myth in this country's background. There are semi-myth figures such as Washington, minor- myth figures such as Paul Bunyan, nonsense-myth figures such as Superman, but there is no Roland, no Arthur, no Siegfried. Oblig- ingly and profitably, sports promoters have thrown their hirelings into the breach. Hollywood offers Ava Gardner as Aphrodite; sports gives us Babe Ruth as Zeus." (Page 267). Kahn, R. (1958). Money, muscles—and myths. In *Mass leisure (*E. Larrabee & R. Meyersohn, Eds.). Glencoe, IL: The Free Press, pp. 264-268.

A hero has been defined as "a man of distinguished courage or ability admired for his brave deeds and noble qualities," whereas a culture hero is explained as "a mythicized historical figure who embodies the aspirations or ideals of a society." If we seek to name a United States sport hero and place him or her in cultural perspective in the first half of the 20th century, a great many people would immediately name Babe Ruth as a culture hero in the post-World War I era.

Conversely, through a sin of omission, as I see it, our society rates much lower—to a truly significant degree—another outstanding professional athlete on the same team who contributed at least equally to the team's win-loss record in those glory years. However, Gehrig made these accomplishments in a quiet, unassuming, gentlemanly, and sportsmanlike manner. Imagine this: in a recent survey of 31 sport historians, 29 of the group selected Ruth as the greatest sport figure in

American history. Thus, whereas Ruth ranked first, Gehrig ranked <u>28</u> of the 31 sport figures who were named (Correspondence with **D. L. Porter**, 1983).

I was forced to ask myself how this could happen in a country with the espoused values and ideals of the United States. Just think about our history and the people whose memories we have come to cherish. Now, answer this series of questions keeping these two athletes in mind. Who came from a poor background and yet worked his way through college? (Of course, Ruth came from a very modest background, as did Gehrig.) Who was a ruggedly handsome young man? Who was shy and modest? Who neither drank nor chased women, and who never broke curfew? Who played 2,130 consecutive, complete baseball games for 14 consecutive years despite "'beanings', fractures of toes and fingers, fevers, torn tendons, sprained ankles, pulled muscles, lumbago, colds, and other mishaps" (Gallico, 1942, p. 87)? Who was characterized by Ty Cobb as "the 'hustlinest' ball play I ever saw" (p. 88)? (This was no mean compliment coming from one who probably deserved that accolade himself !)

Who practiced unbelievably hard to correct his fielding deficiencies at first base? Who took care of his poor, old mother on the way up, and also when he was suc-cessful (the lady who had been the cook and maid at his Columbia University fra-ternity house? Who batted in the clean-up (No. 4) spot in the line-up of the "mighty Yankees?" Who forced opposing pitchers to pitch to Babe Ruth (batter no. 3), rather than walk him) because they knew they would be facing Gehrig next? Who matched Ruth homer for homer right down to the wire in that year (and ended up with 47 himself) when Ruth established his outstanding record of 60 home runs? Finally, and this list of questions could be extended, who—despite Ruth's accomplishment—was voted the most valuable player in the American League by the sportswriters in that same year of 1927? The answer to all of these questions is Lou Gehrig!

If this assessment of the situation is correct, what does this tell us about the United States and the millions of sports fans? What does this tell us about athletes and highly competitive sport in our culture? Was sport a "socially useful servant" then, and can it still be regarded as such today? If sport is <u>not</u> really an important, useful social force today, what good is it anyhow? (Is it enough, for example, for sport to serve as entertainment or an escape from daily responsibilities?) Further, why do we condone some of the shameful and often illegal actions of athletes, and then turn right around and condemn similar behavior by non-athletes in everyday life?

I believe that this is a highly important matter about which intelligent, influential people must become increasingly concerned. For better or worse, competitive sport <u>is</u> becoming an increasingly important social force in the world—almost too great an influence. The daily misconduct that is permitted (and often condoned and publicized) on the part of spectators, athletes, coaches, and administrators in both professional, semiprofessional, and amateur

In this paper I have argued that Lou Gehrig, the Babe's teammate, is actually the person who should have been so named—and that this recognition should have carried through to the present. Crepeau in writing about the "tensions of the twenties" viewed this decade "as an important watershed in the development of the United States." In commenting about George Herman Ruth, he stated: "Ruth is the essence of the rugged individual playing the national game of the cow pasture in an urban stadium before the cheering masses of the machine age." Building on this statement that seems to epitomize the early 20th century growth of the world's largest and most powerful capitalistic democracy, it becomes understandable why a number of philosophers and other critics have argued that the United States has had "an idealistic superstructure and a materialistic base!" If this is true, it is probably nowhere more evident than in the way that Babe Ruth and Lou Gehrig, two of the more important "elements" who made up the "Pride of the Yankees," have been looked upon by average citizens then and down to the present.

"The Babe" has become a culture hero of the greatest magnitude despite the very obvious, serious flaws in his character, while "Larrupin' Lou," Ruth's teammate, is only remembered fondly by some baseball aficionados as an excellent durable athlete with many fine personality traits. What we have here, I maintain, is a situation where history has given a much higher rating to an outstanding professional athlete who possessed a disproportionate amount of arrogance and flair for the dramatic, traits that were coupled with other character flaws that flaunted the avowed values of the nation, whereas it (history) rates much lower—to a most significant degree—another outstanding professional athlete on the same team who contributed *at least equally* to the Yankees' success in those glory years, but who did it in a quiet, unassuming, gentlemanly, and sportsmanlike manner. If this assessment of the situation is correct, what does it tell us about athletes and sport in our culture?

Also, what does it tell us about the United States and its people? If this is what happens in competitive sport, we might ask if highly competitive sport was indeed a "socially useful servant" then, and if it still can be regarded as such today? If it weren't regarded as such then, and it still isn't today, what good is it anyhow? Or is it possible that we condone certain actions in sport and athletics at any level, and turn right around and condemn similar behavior in everyday life? I believe that this is a highly important matter about which intelligent, influential people must become very concerned in the near future.

Competitive sport is becoming an increasingly important social force in the world—almost too great an influence if this is possible. Further, culture heroes are truly hard to come by these days. If we really want the United States to be the finest of nations in *all* regards, and if we really feel that sport has an important contribution to make to the development of such a society, I believe it is time to give the highest reward and acclaim to whose who demonstrate through sport *both a* high degree of athletic ability *and* the finest of personality and character traits. If we were functioning according to such a criterion, it would be Gehrig who is the folk hero today, and Ruth who is remembered as the "home run king" with the badly flawed character and personality. Frankly, I don't believe that this position is clear in the minds of most citizens, young or old. Scott Silvers, of Kansas City, Missouri, in a letter to *Sports Illustrated* (Oct. 29, 1984) about Walter Payton's new rushing record in professional football, stated; "I'm sure that many of your readers will be nominating him for Sportsman of the Year. Nobody deserves it more... The term 'Sportsman' implies traits that go beyond athleticism: humility, kindness, generosity" (p. 110). If this be true, a true "sportsman of the year" is someone who combines these fine personal attributes with outstanding athletic accomplishment. I believe that Lou Gehrig fulfilled these criteria superbly. The Babe did not. I rest my case.

# America Is Screwing Up Physical (Activity) Education and (Educational) Sport

*Note: These 20 "ways" were assembled because John Tirman's in his 100 Ways That America Is Screwing Up the World (NY: Harper Perennial, 2006) did not touch upon my major professional interest.*

1. Allowing "trash talk" in competitive sport.

2. Promoting the idea that "**WINNING**" is the only thing…

3. Permitting "showboating" by athletes after a successful play.

4. Spending infinitely more money on varsity sports for the very few than is spent on intramural sports for the **overwhelming** majority

5. The offering of "athletic scholarships" when there is no "financial need".

6. Permitting "TV sport universities" to debase education by their promotion of semi-professional sport played by so-called "scholar-athletes".

7. Permitting professional boxing (brain damage!) (Or amateur boxing—unless special protection is available.)

8. Featuring professional wrestling on television (a disgusting travesty…)

9. Permitting "all-out" combat ("Extreme Sport") on TV—Now for women too!

10. Permitting (promoting?) the increasing development of "high-risk" sport where "life and limb" are increasingly threatened.

11. Promoting the idea that competitive sport is good for young people, but then **denying** funding for intramural sport in the schools.

12. Permitting professional boxing as a sport for women too!

13. Encouraging the whole idea of "martial-art" sport—when it's "self-defense" that should be stressed—not aggression!

14. Failing to take action sooner—and more strongly!—against drugs in sport. This abuse is "killing" it at all levels.

15. Permitting the type of sport in which studies have shown **fair play, honesty, and sportsmanship actually decline in a university experience** (Stoll et al.).

16. Paying ridiculously high salaries to professional athletes thus creating a "false sense of values" to youth.

17. Permitting the concept of "hero" to be applied to professional athletes unworthy of such ascription thus unduly influencing youth as to what's important in life.

18. Overemphasizing the importance of involvement (and winning!) in international sport competition. ("Own the podium" mentality)

19. Permitting the expansion of "violent" sports, but not also making appropriate provisions for excellent "sport injury care" for all.

20. Fostering a way of life that encourages "spectatoritis" instead of actual ongoing involvement in healthful physical activity and sport.

# A Clash of Moral and Socio-Instrumental Values: Tiger Woods Caught In a Vise

Tiger Woods, named the outstanding golf professional of the 2000-2009 decade and undoubtedly a "golden boy" in the sporting world, has been leading a double life. Presumably happily married to a beautiful Swedish wife with two lovely children, and on the way to becoming fabulously wealthy, Woods had an automobile accident outside of his home in the early hours of a morning. This mishap subsequently brought to light a tale of extraordinary, "extracurricular" sexual activity with many mistresses far and wide.

This scandal immediately became one of the top media stories of the year 2009. The public was surprised and also startled. In fairly short order, the "miscreant" felt constrained to offer a public apology and to take an indefinite leave from his work as professional golf player. The implications resulting from this move away from the "world of golf " were potentially devastating to both the future of Woods himself and to the development of the sport of golf.

Watching this scandal mature over several months, I asked myself: "Why was this such a 'big deal'?" Is this development so unusual in the history of the world? Haven't various media personalities, including sport figures, experienced problems of this type before? Why is this particular incident worthy of all this attention?

(Note: The ethical aspect of his relationship with Dr. Galea in To- ronto who administered PEDs in Toronto to speed up Tiger's re- covery from knee surgery is not considered here.) The answer is that this incident is not unique, but it is *unusual. Yet, one wonders why has so much public attention been given to this particular situation? I believe the answer can be found in the fact that, over the past one hundred years, the role of sport in society has changed most radi- cally. Competitive sport has gradually, but steadily, become a social institution that some- how because of capitalism, politics, and money surged enormously in importance. Hence, it has become an extremely powerful social force that must be reckoned with from here into the indeterminate future.*

Because of this upsurge in sport's development, I have personally been attempting to analyze it from a socio-cultural perspective. It appears to be a question of the "use of " and the "abuse of " of sport. The underlying theoretical argument that can be made is as follows: Strong institutions (i.e., "forces" or "influences") govern society. Among those social institutions are:

(1) society's values (including created norms based on these values),

(2) the type of political state in vogue,

(3) the prevailing economic system,

(4) the religious beliefs present, etc.

To these longstanding institutions, I have over the years added such other influences as education, the communication media, science and technological advancement, concern for peace, *and now sport itself.* Of all of these, the **values** a society holds, and the accompanying norms developed on the basis of these values, form the strongest institution of all!

## Challenging the Role of Sport in Society

In "the Tiger Woods Saga", we find Tiger as a prominent figure in sport, a social institution whose influence has increased phenomenally. This development has become so vast that we may now ask whether it is accomplishing what it is presumably supposed to do. Is highly competitive sport as a social phenomenon doing more good than harm in society? The world seems to have accepted as fact that it is! Yet the world community does not really know whether this contention is true or not. Sport's expansion is permitted and encouraged almost without question in all quarters. "Sport is good for people, and more involvement with sport of almost any type—extreme sport, professional wrestling, missed martial arts, 'world cups'—even watching it regularly (!)—is better" seems to be the conventional wisdom. Witness, in addition, the billions of dollars that are being removed neatly out of tax revenues for the several Olympic enterprises perennially.

As I analyzed the "Tiger Woods Saga," I found it impossible to avoid a critique of commercialized sport as well. I believe that the development is now such that society should be striving to keep sport's drawbacks and/or excesses in check to the greatest possible extent. In recent decades we have witnessed the rise of sport throughout the land to the status of a fundamentalist religion. For example, we find sport being called upon to serve as a "redeemer of wayward youth," but—as it is occurring elsewhere—I believe it is also becoming a destroyer of certain fundamental values of individual and social life.

Wilcox, for example, in his empirical analysis, challenged "the widely held notion that sport can fulfill an important role in the development of national character." He stated: "the assumption that sport is conducive to the development of positive human values, or the 'building of character,' should be viewed more as a belief rather than as a fact." He concluded that sport did "provide some evidence to support a relationship between participation in sport and the ranking of human values" (1991, pp. 3, 17, 18, respectively).

Assuming Wilcox's view has reasonable validity, those involved in any way in the institution of sport—if they all together may be considered a collectivity—should contribute a quantity of redeeming social value to our North American culture, not to mention the overall world culture (i.e., a quantity of good leading to improved societal well-being). On the basis of this argument, the following two questions can be postulated for response by concerned agencies and individuals (e.g., federal governments, state and provincial officials, philosophers in the discipline and related professions):

(1) Can, does, or should a great (i.e., leading) nation produce great sport?

(2) With the world being threatened environmentally in a variety of ways, should we now be considering the "ecology" of sport as we are doing with

other human activity? Both the beneficial and disadvantageous aspects of a particular sporting activity should be studied through the endeavors of scholars in various disciplines as well?

(3) If it is indeed the case that the guardian of the "functional satisfaction" resulting from sport is (a) the sports person, (b) the spectator, (c) the business-person who gains monetarily, (d) the sport manager, and, in some instances, (e) educational administrators and their respective governing boards, then who in society should be in a position to be the most knowledgeable about the immediate objectives and long range aims of sport and related physical activity?

Answering these questions is a complex matter. First, as stated above, sport and related physical activity have become an extremely powerful social force in society. Secondly, if we grant that sport now has significant power in almost all of the world's developed cultures—a power indeed that appears to be growing—we should also recognize that any such social force affecting society is dangerous if perverted (e.g., through an excess of nationalism or commercialism). With this in mind, I am stating further that sport has somehow achieved such status as a powerful societal institution without an adequately defined underlying theory. Somehow, most countries seem to be proceeding generally on a typically unstated assumption that "sport is a good thing for society to encourage, and *more* sport is even better!" And yet, as explained above, the term "sport" exhibits radical ambiguity based on both everyday usage and dictionary definition. This obviously adds even more to the present problem and accompanying confusion.

This "radical ambiguity" about the role of sport takes us back to "the Tiger Woods Saga". Sport has now become a powerful social institution exerting influence for the betterment of society. Then, all of a sudden, a "sport hero" of the highest magnitude behaves himself in such a way that basic societal values are challenged. Hence, we now must ask ourselves: "Specifically what are *the* values that Tiger has forsaken that have occasioned this world-wide outburst of publicity"?

## "Socio-Instrumental" Values or "Moral" Values?

Examining this matter carefully, we may be surprised to learn that sport's contribution to human wellbeing is a highly complicated matter. On the one side, there are those who claim that sport contributes significantly to the development of what are regarded as the *socio-instrumental* values—that is, the values of teamwork, loyalty, self-sacrifice, aggressiveness, and perseverance consonant with prevailing corporate capitalism in democracy and in most other political systems as well. In the process of making this "contribution," however, we discover also that there is now a good deal of evidence that in the process of contributing to the "global ideal" of capitalism, democracy, and advancing technology, sport has developed an ideal that opposes the historical, fundamental *moral* values of honesty, fairness, good will, sportsmanship, and responsibility in the innumerable competitive experiences provided (Lumpkin, Stoll, and Beller, 1999).

Significant to this discussion are the results of investigations carried out by Hahm, Stoll, Beller, Rudd, and others in recent years. The Hahm-Beller Choice Inventory (HBVCI) has now been administered to athletes at different levels in a variety of venues. It demonstrates conclusively that athletes are increasingly *not* supporting what is considered "the moral ideal" in competition. As Stoll and Beller (1998) reported, for example, an athlete with moral character demonstrates the moral character traits of honesty, fair play, respect, and responsibility whether an official is present to enforce the rules or not. (Priest, Krause, and Beach substantiated this finding in 1999). They reported that changes over a four-year period in a college athlete's ethical value choices were consistent with other investigations. Their findings showed *decreases* in "sportsmanship orientation" and an *increase* in "professional" attitudes associated with sport bespeaking so-called "social" values.

Aha! We have now arrived at the nub of the matter! Alas for poor Tiger Woods… His plight is that he is "caught" right in the middle of this ongoing controversy about the presumed contribution of sport. No matter which way he turns, he is "out of step" with the claims for sport made by either group. His actions clash with those who say that sport contributes to *socio-instrumental* values. In addition, they also clash with those who argue that sport contributes to *moral* values. The perennial winner in golf, poor Tiger can't win now for losing! On the one hand he has confounded those who argue for "the social-values contribution", and—on the other hand—he has betrayed those who promote sport because it makes "a moral-values contribution". Hence, some of his advertisers are now deserting Tiger because his commercial value to them has been tarnished perhaps irrevocably. The gross stock value of his many sponsors has decreased appreciably since Tiger has been exposed. Concurrently, the sports *hero*, that staunch fellow presumably with all of those fine moral values, has betrayed his fans young and old because of his "nocturnal peregrinations." Woe is Tiger!

## Concluding Statement

Even though dictionaries define *social* character similarly, many sport practitioners, including participants, coaches, parents, and officials, have gradually come to believe that character is defined properly by such values as self-sacrifice, teamwork, loyalty, and perseverance. The common expression in competitive sport is: "He or she showed character"—meaning "He/she 'hung in there' to the bitter end!" [or whatever...]. Rudd (1999) confirmed that coaches explained character as "work ethic and commitment." This coincides with what sport sociologists have found. Sage (1998. p. 614) explained: "Mottoes and slogans such as 'sports builds character' must be seen in the light of their ideological issues." In other words, competitive sport is structured by the nature of the society in which it occurs. This would appear to mean that over-commercialization, drug-taking, cheating, bribe- taking by officials, violence, etc. at all levels of sport are simply reflections of the culture in which we live.

Robert Osterhoudt (2010), one of the world's leading sport philosophers, offers a fundamental distinction to this troubling development as follows:

> ... it does seem to me as well that such social values as earnest effort, dedication, self-sacrifice, and the like are meaningfully talked about in respect to sport and become defensible features of it *only if* they occur in the service of sport's inherent character as playful, competitive, and physical, not if they occur in the service of other forms of aim, such as commercial, nationalist, or military aim in particular. *The most fundamental distinction in all of this is thus the dividing of intrinsic and instrumental values, not the dividing of moral and social values.* (This is

so because moral values, as described, serve *inherently*, thus becoming distinctly human ends.)

Where does all of this leave us today as we consider sport's presumed relationship with both *moral* character development and with *socio-instrumental* character development? Whatever your conclusion may be, Tiger Woods has been unexpectedly trapped in this "socio-instrumental" versus "moral" character vise that characterizes sport participation at the beginning of the 21ˢᵗ century. He tried to have it both ways. For his and his family's sake, let us hope that he will learn from this tragic experience—and that "the world" will "forgive his sins"…

# Semi-ProfessIonal Sport Does Not a Great University Make

*Note: This article was published in the CAUT Bulletin, Vol. 56, No. 7, June 2008. The views expressed are those of the author and not necessarily CAUT.*

When I came to Canada in 1949, four university football teams were playing in the Senior Intercollegiate Football League that existed at the time in Central Canada — Toronto, McGill, Queen's and Western Ontario. At Western, John Metras was head coach, Dr. Jack Fairs was backfield coach and I served as line coach. Happily, Western emerged as Canadian champions in both 1949-1950 and 1950-1951.

How times have changed. The official rankings indicate none of the football teams from these four universities are now listed in the top 10. These four universities have presumably maintained their academic standards for student admission and retention — and are not "buying" student-athletes in one way or another just to win games.

Should the present lowly status of the "Big Four" universities vis-à-vis national football standing concern us? It has been reported that Nero fiddled while Rome burned. But then we are not certain he had all of his mental faculties. I would argue we too are "fiddling" while some aspects of university competitive sport are catching fire.

Truly, it is not fair to athletes and coaches when they do well within one league, to have them advance to national play-downs competing with teams from other conferences where athletic scholarships or other financial enticements are the norm. We want our athletes to continue to do the best they can within an educational environment. Semiprofessional sport does not a great university make.

At this time, several potential box-office university sports are gradually sliding into semi-professionalism. I have no quarrel with a young person striving for excellence in competitive sport on a semiprofessional or professional basis. Sport is a legitimate aspect of our culture despite the abuses that are increasingly part of the scene.

Unfortunately, cheating and deceit are what have developed with semi- professionalism in the 20th century for so many young people in commercialized American university sport. These athletes are often underprivileged youngsters who spend so much time on football, for example, that they rarely earn a baccalaureate degree in the allotted four years. I am worried this "U.S. cancer" will spread north of the border.

Because of the excessive pressure exerted when semi-professionalism in university sport is allowed, there are now reportedly more than 400 substances that may be ingested as many coaches and athletes seek improved performance. Anabolic steroids are just the tip of the iceberg. We shouldn't increasingly place our Canadian university athletes in such a position that, because of pressure to win, they are tempted to experiment with potentially harmful drugs.

Canada generally has done quite well until now. High school instructors and coaches in Canada have, by and large, preserved athletics of an educational nature in their programs for students. Undoubtedly there's been much support from principals and superintendents. I worry that Canadian university and college administrators won't continue to show as much sense—that they may be unduly swayed by wealthy alumni, or government, that from time to time seem determined to use universities as training grounds for international elite sport.

Our problem is that there are conflicting forces at work within our federal government and universities that are gradually leading us down the garden path to a Canadian version of the "scholar-athlete," as identified by both the U.S. National Collegiate Athletic Association and the National Association for Intercollegiate

Athletics. Many of our Canadian officials and administrators argue that we are too intelligent and wise to allow the worst elements of the U.S. system to develop within higher education here. This may be true, but I doubt it.

I taught and coached at Yale and from 1961-63 administered the physical education department in education at Michigan and the department of physical education at Illinois from 1963-1970. I know what developed there. So when I had the opportunity to return to Canada as the first dean of the faculty of physical education at Western in the early 1970s, I heaved a great sigh of relief. I was happy to return to a situation in which the new faculty's undergraduate program, graduate program, intercollegiate athletics program and physical recreation and intramural program were "all under the same roof ", and thus I could strive for a concept of "balanced excellence" in an educational environment.

Now, 40 years later, the situation in higher education has changed markedly in all parts of the country. Western University has truly been favored because of the quality of its athletic administrators and coaches since the program started. Many individuals have contributed to this unique development. Today, because of social forces and certain professional concerns within the field, we're at a crossroad.

University administrators and faculty members across the land need to be kept on alert to the growing, insidious influence of the media barrage emanating from all over America covering the exploits of the majority of universities and colleges where semiprofessional athletics prevails.

As matters are progressing now, the best hope for retention of athletic sanity for some Canadian universities (e.g., those relating to Ontario interuniversity athletics) would be the establishment of a Canadian "Ivy League." This would leave an assortment of other institutions in the East, West and Quebec selling their "academic souls" for a mess of pottage in a wide-open Canadian league. But, how do the resultant media attention and notoriety of such present endeavor benefit them? Winning football teams may attract attention, but they do not make a great university.

Canadian universities should be wiser than their commercialized U.S. counterparts are with their overall sport programs. Our objective should be solely to profit from the benefits that a sound program of developmental physical activity in sport, exercise and related expressive activities can bring for all people in our country—accelerated, normal, or special.

Canada can do reasonably well in international sport as well as provide healthful physical activity and physical recreation for all its citizens. Achieving such a balance can be done without perverting secondary or higher education. At the university level, we have a sufficient number of problems while we strive to avoid shabbiness because of inadequate support.

Allowing an increasing, unhealthy type of athletic-scholarship mentality to creep into university sport would eventually make us laughable to those who truly understand how it "ought to be." It would also have a deleterious effect at the lower educational levels.

It's better to be proud and somewhat poorer financially, yet remain honorable and fair as we promote educational and recreational sport for all of our students.

## On What Basis Might a Country Sponsor the Olympic Games?

There's a vocal minority who believe the Olympic Games should be abolished. There's another minority, including the Games officials and the athletes, who presumably feel the enterprise is doing just fine. There's a larger minority undoubtedly solidly behind the commercial aspects of the undertaking. They have a good thing going; they liked the Games the way they are developing—the bigger, the better! Finally, there's the vast majority to whom the Olympics are either interesting, somewhat interesting, or a bore. This "vast majority," if the Games weren't there every four years, would probably agree that the world would go on just the same, and some other social phenomenon would take up their leisure time.

The people love a spectacle. The 2000 Olympic Games held in Sydney, Australia were a spectacle, from start to finish. Sydney, Australia evidently wanted worldwide recognition. Without doubt, Sydney got recognition! The world's outstanding athletes wanted the opportunity to demonstrate their excellence. From all reports they had such an occasion to their heart's and ability's content. The International Olympic Committee, along with their counterparts in each of the

200 participating nations, earnestly desired the show to go on; it went on with a bang! Obviously, Sydney spent an enormous amount of money and energy to finance and otherwise support this extravaganza and surrounding competition. The IOC and its affiliates will presumably remain solvent for another four years, while Sydney contemplates its involvement with this enormous event and its aftermath. "Problem, what problem?" most people in the public sector would assuredly ask if they were confronted with such a question.

## The Problem

This analysis revolves around the criticisms of the "abolish the Games group." Sir William Rees-Mogg (1988, pp. 7-8), is one of the Olympic Movement's most vituperative opponents. He believes the problem is of enormous magnitude. In fact, he lists fifteen sub—problems in no particular order of importance except for the first criticism that sets the tone for the remainder: "The Olympic Games have become a grotesque jamboree of international hypocrisy. Whatever idealism they once had has been lost. The Games now stand for some of the things which are most rotten and corrupt in the modern world, for prestige, nationalism, publicity, prejudice, bureaucracy, and the exploitation of talent" (p. 7).

It would not be appropriate to enumerate here *in great detail* the remaining 14 problems and issues brought forward by Rees-Mogg. Simply put, however, he states: "The Games have been taken over by a vulgar nationalism, in place of the spirit of internationalism for which they were revived" (p.7). He decries also that, in addition to promoting racial intolerance, "the objectives of many national Olympic programmes is the glorification and self-assertion of totalitarian state regimes," often "vile regimes guilty of many of the crimes which the Olympic Games are supposed to outlaw" (p. 7).

Rees-Mogg decries further "The administration of the Olympic Games [that] is politically influenced and morally bankrupt" (p. 7). Additionally, at this point, he asserts: "the international bureaucracies of several sports have become among the most odious of the world." In this respect he lashes out especially at tennis, chess, cricket, and track and field. Still further, he charges that threats by countries to boycott the Olympics have time and again made it a political arena akin to the United Nations.

The messenger has not yet completed his message. Rees-Mogg condemns "the worship of professionally abnormal muscular development," and states that it is "a form of idolatry to which ordinary life is often sacrificed" (p. 7). Since these words were written in 1988, these problems have assuredly not been corrected. They have actually worsened (e.g., ever-more drugs to enhance performance, bribery of officials assigned to site selection). The entire problem of drug ingestion to promote bodily development for enhanced performance has now become legendary. Couple this with over-training begun at early ages in selected sports for both boys and girls, and it can be argued safely that *natural*, all-round development has been thwarted for a great many young people, not to mention the fact that only a minute number makes it through to "Olympic glory." More could be said, but the point has been made. Basically, Rees-Mogg has claimed that it has become a world "in which good *values* are taken by dishonest men and put to shameful uses" (p. 8).

## An Assessment of the Problem.

The problem, the author believes, is this: opportunities for participation in all competitive sport—not just *Olympic* sport— moved historically from amateurism to semi-professionalism, and then on to full-blown professionalism. The Olympic Movement, because of a variety of social pressures, followed suit in both ancient times and in the present. When the International Olympic Committee gave that final push to the pendulum and openly admitted professional athletes to play in the Games, they may have pleased most of the spectators and all of the advertising and media representatives. But in so doing the floodgates were opened completely, and the original ideals upon which the Games were reactivated were completely abandoned. This is what caused Sir Rees-Mogg to state that crass commercialism had won the day. This final abandonment of any semblance of what was the original Olympic ideal was the "straw that broke the camel's back." This ultimate decision regarding eligibility for participation has indeed been devastating to those people who earnestly believe that money and sport are like oil and water; they simply do not mix! Their response has been to abandon any further interest in, or support for, the entire Olympic Movement.

The question must, therefore be asked: "What should rampant professionalism in competitive sport at the Olympic Games mean to any given country out of the 200 nations involved?" This is not a simple question to answer responsibly. In this present brief statement, it should be made clear that the professed social values of a country *should* ultimately prevail—and they *will* prevail in the final analysis. However, this ultimate determination will not take place overnight. The *fundamental social values* of a social system will eventually have a strong influence on the *individual values* held by most citizens in that country, also. If a country is moving toward the most important twin values of equalitarianism and achievement, for example, what implications does that have for competitive sport in that political entity under consideration? The following are some questions that should be asked *before* a strong continuing commitment is made to sponsor such involvement through governmental and/or private funding:

1. *Can it be shown that* involvement in competitive sport atones or the other of the three levels (i.e., amateur, semiprofessional, professional) brings about desirable *social* values (i.e., more value than disvalue)?

2. *Can it be shown that* involvement in competitive sport at one or the other of the three levels (i.e., amateur, semiprofessional, or professional) brings about desirable *individual* values of both an *intrinsic* and *extrinsic* nature (i.e., creates more value than disvalue)?

3. *If the answer to Questions #1 and #2 immediately are both affirmative* (i.e., that involvement in competitive sport at any or all of the three levels postulated [i.e., *amateur, semiprofessional, and professional* sport] provides a sufficient amount of social and individual value to warrant such promotion), can sufficient funds be made available to support or permit this promotion at any or all of the three levels listed?

4. *If funding to support participation in competitive sport at any or all of the three levels (amateur, semiprofessional, professional) is not available (or such participation is*

*not deemed advisable), should priorities—as determined by the expressed will of the people—be established about the importance of each level to the country based on careful analysis of the potential social and individual values that may accrue to the society and its citizens from such competitive sport participation at one or more levels?*

## Concluding Statement

In this analysis I asked whether a country should be involved with, or continue involvement with, the ongoing Olympic Movement—as well as *all* competitive sport—unless the people in that country first answer some basic questions. These questions ask to what extent such involvement can be related to the social and individual values that the country holds as important for all of its citizens. Initially, study will be needed to determine whether sport competition at either or all of the three levels (i.e., amateur, semi-professional, and professional) does indeed provide positive social and individual value (i.e., more value than disvalue) in the country concerned. Then careful assessment—through the efforts of qualified social scientists and philosophers—should be made of the populace's opinions and basic beliefs about such involvement. If participation in competitive sport at each of the three levels can make this claim to being a social institution that provides positive value to the country, these efforts should be supported to the extent possible— including the sending of a team to future Olympic Games. If sufficient funding for the support of *all* three levels of participation is *not* available, from either governmental or private sources, *the expressed will of the people should be established to determine what priorities will be invoked.*

## References

Berelson, B. and Steiner, G. A. (1964). *Human Behavior.* NY: Harcourt, Brace, Jovanovich.

Borgman, A. (1993) *Crossing the Postmodern Divide.* Chicago: The University of Chicago Press.

Commager, H.S. (1961). A quarter century—Its advances. *Look*, 25, 10 (June 6), 80-91.

Cousins, N. (1974). Prophecy and pessimism. *Saturday Review WORLD*, Aug/ 24, 6-7.

Huntington, S. P. (June 6, 1993). World politics entering a new phase, *The New York Times*, E19

Lipset. S. M. (1973). National Character. In D. Koulack & D. Perlman (Eds.), *Readings in Social Psychology: Focus on Canada.* Toronto: Wiley.

Marx, L. (1990). Does improved technology mean progress? In Teich, A. H. (Ed.), *Technology and the Future.* NY: St. Martin's Press.

Michael, D.N. (1962). Cybernation: the silent conquest. Santa Barbara, CA: Center for the Study of Democratic Institutions.

Naisbitt, J. (1982). *Megatrends.* New York: Warner.

Naisbitt, J. & Aburdene, P. (1990). *Megatrends* 2000. New York: Wm. Morrow.

Rorty, R. (1997) *Achieving Our Country.* Cambridge, MA: Harvard University Press

Ten events that shook the world between 1984 and 1994. (Special Report). *Utne Reader*, 62 (March/April 1994): 58.

# Sport in the Postmodern World

In retrospect, the adventure of civilization began to make some headway because of now-identifiable forms of early striving which embodied elements of great creativity (e.g., the invention of the wheel, the harnessing of fire). The subsequent development in technology, very slowly but steadily, offered humans some surplus of material goods over and above that needed for daily living. For example, the early harnessing of nature created the irrigation systems of Sumeria and Egypt, and these accomplishments led to the establishment of the first cities. Here material surpluses were collected, managed, and sometimes squandered; nevertheless, necessary early accounting methods were created that were subsequently expanded in a way that introduced writing to the human scene. As we now know, the development of this form of communication in time helped humans expand their self-consciousness and to evolve gradually and steadily in all aspects of culture. For better or worse, however, the end result of this social and material progress has created a mixed agenda characterized by good and evil down to the present. The world's blanketing communications network has now exceeded humankind's ability to cope with it.

Muller (1952) concluded, "the adventure of civilization is necessarily inclusive" (p. 53). By that he meant that evil will probably always be with humankind to some degree, but it is civilization that sets the standards and accordingly works to eradicate at least the worst forms of such evil. Racial prejudice, for example, must be overcome. For better or worse, there are now more than six billion people on earth, and that number appears to be growing faster than the national debt!

These earth creatures are black-, yellow-, brown-, or white-skinned, but fundamentally we now know from genetic research that there is an "overwhelming oneness" in all humankind that we dare not forget in our overall planning (Huxley, 1957).

As various world evils are overcome, or at least held in check, scientific and accompanying technological development will be called upon increasingly to meet the demands of the exploding population. Gainful work and a reasonable amount of leisure will be required for further development. Unfortunately, the necessary leisure required for the many aspects of a broad, societal culture to develop fully, as well as for an individual to grow and develop similarly within it, has come slowly. The average person in the world is far from a full realization of such benefits. Why "the good life" for all has been so slow in arriving is not an easy question to answer. Of course, we might argue that times do change slowly, and that the possibility of increased leisure has really come quite rapidly—once humans began to achieve some control of their environment.

## Naipaul or Huntington: "Universal Civilization or the Clash of Civilizations?

Naipaul (1990) had theorized that we are developing a "universal civilization" characterized by (1) the sharing of certain basic values, (2) what their societies have in common (e.g., cities and literacy, (3) certain of the attributes of Western civilization (e.g., market economies and political democracy), and (4) consumption patterns (e.g., fads) of Western civilization. Samuel Huntington (1998), the eminent political scientist, doesn't see this happening, however, although he does see some merit in these arguments. He grants that Western civilization is different than any other civilization that has ever existed because of its marked impact on the whole world since 1500. However, he doesn't know whether the West will be able to reverse the signs of decay already present and thus renew itself.

Sadly, there have been innumerable wars throughout history with very little if any let-up down to the present. Nothing is so devastating to a country's economy as war. Now, whether we like it or not, the world is gradually sliding into what Huntington has designated as "the clash of civilizations." Some people have seized upon his analysis as a justification for the United States to move still further in the War on Terrorism by the installation of what has euphemistically been called a "modernized regime" in Iraq. It is argued that this "accomplishment" would help toward the gradual achievement of worldwide democratic values along with global capitalism and so-called free markets.

The Misreading of Huntington's Thought. This misreading of Huntington's thought, however, needs to be corrected. As it stands, he asserts, "Western belief in the universality of Western culture suffers three problems... It is false; it is immoral; and it is dangerous" (p. 310). He believes strongly that these religion-based cultures, such as the Islamic and the Chinese, should be permitted to find their own way in the 21st century. In fact, they will probably do so anyhow, no matter what the West does. Then individually (hopefully not together!), they will probably each become superpowers themselves. The "unknown quality" of their future goals will undoubtedly fuel the desires of those anxious for the United States to maintain overwhelming military superiority along with continually expanding technological capability.

While this is going on, however, the United States needs to be more aware of its own internal difficulties. It has never solved its "inner-city problem," along with increases in antisocial behavior generally (i.e., crime, drugs, and violence). Certainly the decay of the traditional family has long-term implications as well. Huntington refers further to a "general weakening of the work ethic and rise of a cult of personal indulgence (p. 304). Still further, there is a definite decline in learning and intellectual activity as indicated by lower levels of academic achievement creating a need for course grade "aggrandizement" (i.e., the gentleman's "C" is "history"). Finally, there has been a marked lessening of "social capital" (the amount of "volunteering" including personal trust in others to meet individual needs).

*Schlesinger's Analysis of America.* These conflicting postulations by Huntington and Naipaul are stated here merely to warn that the present "missionary culture" of the United States is, in many ways, not really a true culture anyhow. So states Arthur Schlesinger, Jr. (1998), the distinguished historian. He points out that in recent years the U.S.A. has gradually acquired an ever-increasing multi-ethnicity. In his The disuniting of America, he decries the present schisms occurring in the United States. He is most concerned that the melting pot concept formerly so prominent in the States is becoming a "Tower of Babel" concept—just like Canada!

He understands, however, that "Canadians have never developed a strong sense of what it is to be a Canadian" by virtue of their dual heritage (p. 17). Huntington explains further that an attempt to export democratic and capitalistic values vigorously to the world's other cultures may be exactly the wrong approach. He believes that they may well be looking mainly for stability in their own traditions and identity. (Japan, for example, has shown the world that it's possible to become "rich and modern" without giving up their illiberal "core identity.") Struggle as all cultures do for renewal when internal decay sets in, no civilization has proven that it is invincible indefinitely. This is exactly why Muller characterized history as somehow being imbued with a "tragic sense."

## The "Tragic Sense" of Life (Muller)

This "tragic sense' that history has displayed consistently was described by Herbert Muller (1952), in his magnificent treatise titled *The uses of the past*. Muller disagrees with the philosopher Hobbes (1588-1679), however, who stated in his *De homine* that very early humans existed in an individual state of nature in which life was anarchic and basically "solitary, poor, nasty, brutish, and short." Muller argued in rebuttal that life "might have been poor and short, but that it was never solitary or simply brutish" (p. 6).

Accordingly, Muller's approach to history was in the spirit of the great tragic poets, a spirit of reverence and/or irony. It is based on the assumption that the tragic sense of life is not only the profoundest, but also the most pertinent for an understanding of both past and present (p. viii).

Muller believed that the drama of human history has been characterized up to now by high tragedy in the Aristotelian sense. As he stated, "all the mighty civilizations have fallen because of tragic flaws; as we are enthralled by any golden age we must always add that it did not last, it did not do" (p. viii). This brings to mind that conceivably the 20th century of the modern era may turn out to have been the "Golden Age" of the United States. As unrealistic as this may sound because I am talking about what today is the most powerful nation in the history of life on Earth, there are also many misgivings developing about the blind optimism concerning history's malleability and compatibility in keeping with American ideals.

"The future as history." More than a generation ago, Heilbroner (1960) arrived at this position similarly. He explained in his "future as history" concept that America's belief in a personal "deity of history" may be shortlived in the 21st century. As he stated this, he emphasized the need to search for a greatly improved "common denominator of values" (p. 170) in the face of technological, political, and economic forces that are "bringing about a closing of our historic future."

As the world turns today in 2002, you may laugh at this prediction. Yet, looking at the situation from a starkly different perspective even earlier, Arnold Toynbee (1947) came to a quite similar conclusion in his monumental A study of history from still another standpoint. He theorized that humankind must return to the one true God from whom it has gradually but steadily fallen away. You can challenge him on this opinion, as I (an agnostic) most assuredly do. Yet, no matter—the ways things are going at present—we on the Earth had best try to use our heads as intelligently and wisely as possible. As we get on with striving to make the world as effective, efficient, and humane as possible, we need to make life as replete with Good, as opposed to Evil, as we possibly can. With this plea for an abundance of righteousness, you may no longer be wondering where this analysis is heading. Let us turn now to what I have termed "the plight" of sport management.

## The "Plight" of Sport Management

At this point, having placed the "adventure of civilization" in some perspective, I will now shift my focus to sport and related physical activity. Here is a societal institution that became an ever-more powerful social force in the 20th century. In this study I am attempting to analyze philosophically and sociologically what I have called reluctantly the "plight" of sport management. Basically, I am arguing that society is governed by strong social forces or institutions. Among those social institutions are (1) the values (and accompanying norms devised) , (2) the type of political state in vogue, (3) the prevailing economic system, (4) the religious beliefs or system present, etc. To these longstanding institutions I have added the influence of such other forces as education, science and technological advancement, concern for peace, and now sport itself. (Zeigler, 1989, Part II) Of these, the values, and the accompanying norms that are developed, form the strongest social institution of all.

***Crossing the Postmodern Divide.*** Whether we all recognize it or not, similar to all other professions today, the burgeoning sport management profession is presently striving to cross what has been termed the postmodern divide. An epoch in civilization approaches closure when many of the fundamental convictions of its advocates are challenged by a substantive minority of the populace. It can be argued that indeed the world is moving into a new epoch as the proponents of postmodernism have been affirming over recent decades. Within such a milieu there are strong indications that sport management is going to have great difficulty crossing this chasm, this so-called, postmodern divide.

A diverse group of postmodern scholars argues that many in democracies, under girded by the various rights being propounded (e.g., individual freedom, privacy), have come to believe that now they too require—and deserve!—a supportive "liberal consensus" within their respective societies. Conservative, essentialist elements prevail at present and are functioning strongly in many Western political systems. With their more authoritative orientation in mind, conservatives believe that the deeper foundation justifying this claim of a need for a more liberal consensus has never been fully rationalized. However, postmodernists now form a substantive minority that supports a more humanistic, pragmatic, liberal consensus in which highly competitive sport is viewed as an increasingly negative influence on society. If this statement is true—there are strong indications that the present sport management profession—as known today—will have difficulty crossing this post-modern divide that has been postulated.

## Characterizations of Competitive Sport

Having stated that "sport" has become a strong social force or institution, it is true also that there has been some ambiguity about what such a simple word means. In an earlier study I recall uncovering that the word "sport" was used in 13 different ways as a noun. Somehow this number has increased to 14 in the most recent Encarta World English Dictionary (1999) (p. 1730). In essence, what we are describing here is an athletic activity requiring skill or physical prowess. It is typically of a competitive nature as in racing, wrestling, baseball, tennis, or cricket. For the people involved, sport is often serious, and participants may even advance to a stage where competitive sport becomes a semi-professional or a professional career choice. For a multitude of others, however, sport is seen more as a diversion, as recreational in nature, and as a pleasant pastime.

A Social Institution Without a Theory. Viewed collectively, I am now arguing that the "totality" of sport appears to have become a strong social institution—but one that is without a well-defined theory. This fact is being recognized increasingly. Yet, at this point the general public, including most politicians, seems to believe that "the more competitive sport we have, the merrier!" I believe, however, that we in the sport management profession need right now to answer such questions as (1) what purposes competitive sport has served in the past, (2) what functions it is fulfilling now, (3) where it seems to be heading, and (4) how it should be employed to serve all humankind.

*How Sport Serves Society* . In response to these questions, without very careful delineation at this point, I believe that sport as presently operative can be subsumed in a non-inclusive list as possibly serving in the following ways:

1. As an organized religion (for those with or without another similar competing affiliation)
2. As an exercise medium (often a sporadic one)
3. As a life-enhancer or "arouser" (puts excitement in life)
4. As a trade or profession (depending upon one's approach to it)

5. As an avocation, perhaps as a "leisure-filler" (at either a passive, vicarious, or active level)

6. As a training ground for war (used throughout history for this purpose)

7. As a "socializing activity" (an activity where one can meet and enjoy friends)

8. As an educational means (i.e., the development of positive character traits, however described)

As I review the list developed above, I find it most interesting that I didn't list "sport as a developer of positive character traits" until last! I wonder why...

My listing could undoubtedly be larger. I could have used such terms as (1) sport "the destroyer," (2) sport "the redeemer," (3) sport "the social institution being tempted by science and technology," (4) sport "the social phenomenon by which heroes and villains are created," or, finally, (5) sport "the social institution that has survived within an era characterized by a vacuum of belief for many." But I must stop. I believe this listing is sufficient to make the necessary point in the present discussion.

I am hoping that you agree that the sport manager truly needs to understand what competitive sport has become in society, as well as why many of its promoters are confronted with a dilemma. I assert this since I believe that sport too—as all other social institutions—is inevitably being confronted by the postmodern divide. In crossing this frontier, many troubling and difficult decisions, often ethical in nature, will have to be made as the professor of sport management seeks to prepare prospective professionals who will guide sport into becoming a responsible social institution. The fundamental question facing the profession is: "What kind of sport do we want to promote to help shape what sort of world in the 21st century?"

## Is Sport Fulfilling Its Presumed Educational and Recreational Roles Adequately?

What implications does all of this have for sport as it enters the 21st century? I believe that there are strong indications that sport's presumed educational and recreational roles in the "adventure" of civilization are not being fulfilled adequately. Frankly, the way commercialized, over-emphasized sport has been operated, it can be added to the list of symptoms of American internal decay enumerated above (e.g., drugs, violence, decline of intellectual interest, dishonesty, greed). If true, this inadequacy inevitably throws a burden on sport management as a profession to do something about it. Sport, along with all of humankind, is facing the postmodern divide.

Reviewing this claim in some detail. Depauw (Quest, 1997) argues that society should demonstrate more concern for those who have traditionally been sex or "physicality"). She speaks of "The (In)Visibility of DisAbility" in our culture. Depauw's position is backed substantively by what Blinde and McCallister (1999) call "The Intersection of Gender and Disability Dynamics."

A second point of contention about sport's contribution relates to the actual "sport experience." The way much sport has been conducted, we have every right to ask, "Does sport build character or 'characters'?" Kavussannu & Roberts (Journal of Sport and Exercise Psychology, 2001) recently showed that, even though "sport participation is widely regarded as an important opportunity for character development," it is also true that sport "occurs in a context that values ego orientation (e.g. winning IS the most important thing)."

***Sport's Contribution Today.*** What is competitive sport's contribution today? If we were to delve into this matter seriously, we might be surprised—or perhaps not. We may well learn that sport is contributing significantly in the development of what are regarded as the social values—that is, the values of teamwork, loyalty, self-sacrifice, and perseverance consonant with prevailing corporate capitalism in democracy and in other political systems as well. Conversely, however, we will also discover that there is now a great deal of evidence that sport may be developing an ideal that opposes the fundamental moral virtues of honesty, fairness, and responsibility in the innumerable competitive experiences provided (Lumpkin, Stoll, and Beller, 1999).

Significant to this discussion are the results of investigations carried out by Hahm, Stoll, Beller, Rudd, and others in recent years. The Hahm-Beller Choice Inventory (HBVCI) has now been administered to athletes at different levels in a variety of venues. It demonstrates conclusively that athletes will not support what is considered "the moral ideal" in competition. As Stoll and Beller (1998) see it, for example, an athlete with moral character demonstrates the moral character traits of  honesty, fair play, respect, and responsibility whether an official is present to enforce the rules or not. This finding was further substantiated by Preist, Krause, and Beach (1999) who reported that their findings in the four-year changes in college athlete's ethical value choices were consistent with other investigations. They showed decreases in "sportsmanship orientation" and an increase in "professional" attitudes associated with sport.

On the other hand, even though dictionaries define social character similarly, sport practitioners, including participants, coaches, parents, and officials, have come to believe that character is defined properly by such values as self-sacrifice, teamwork, loyalty, and perseverance. The common expression in competitive sport is: "He/she showed character"—meaning "He/she 'hung in there' to the bitter end!" [or whatever]. Rudd (1999) confirmed that coaches explained character as "work ethic and commitment." This coincides with what sport sociologists have found. Sage (1998. p. 614) explained that "Mottoes and slogans such as 'sports builds character' must be seen in the light of their ideological issues" In other words, competitive sport is structured by the nature of the society in which it occurs. This would appear to mean that over-commercialization, drug- taking, cheating, bribe-taking by officials, violence, etc. at all levels of sport are simply reflections of the culture in which we live. So much for sport's presumed relationship with moral character development.

At this point, we can't help but recall that the ancient Olympic Games became so excessive with its ills that they were abolished. They were begun again only by the spark provided in the late 19th century byde Coubertin's "noble amateur ideal." The way things are going today, it is not unthinkable that the steadily increasing excesses of the present Olympic Games Movement could well bring about their demise again. However, they are only symptomatic of a larger problem confronting an American culture. Despite its claims to be "the last best hope on earth," American culture appears to be facing what Berman (2000) calls "spiritual death" (p. 52). He makes this claim because of "its crumbling school systems and widespread functional illiteracy, violent crime and gross economic inequality, and apathy and cynicism."

This discussion about whether sport's presumed educational and recreational roles have justification in fact could go on indefinitely. So many negative incidents have occurred that one hardly knows where to turn to avoid further negative examples. On the one hand we read the almost unbelievably high standards set in the Code of Conduct developed by the Coaches Council of the National Association for Sport and Physical Education (NASPE) (2001); yet, conversely we learn that today athletes' concern for the presence of moral values in sport declines over the course of a university career (Priest, Krause, and Beach, 1999).

***Sedentary Living Has Caught Up With Us.*** With this as a backdrop, we learn further that Americans, for example, are increasingly facing the cost and consequences of sedentary living (Booth & Chakravarthy, 2002). Additionally, Malina (2001) tells us that there is a need to track people's physical activity across their lifespans. Finally, Corbin and Pangrazi (2001) explain that we haven't yet been able to devise and accept a uniform definition of wellness for all people. The one thought that emerges from these various assessments is as follows: We give every evidence of wanting our "sport spectaculars" for the few much more than we want all people of all ages and all conditions to have meaningful sport and exercise involvements throughout their lives, for example, described a most recent Environics survey that explained that "65% of Canadians would like more government money spent on local arenas, playgrounds, and swimming pools, as well as on sports for women, the poor, the disabled, and aboriginals." At the same time, Dr. Ayotte, director of the only International Olympic Committee-accredited testing laboratory in Canada, explains that young athletes believe you must take drugs to compete successfully. "People have no faith in hard work and food now," she says, to achieve success in sport (Long, 2001).

## Official Sport's Response to the Prevailing Situation

And where do we find what we often call "sport officialdom" responding to this situation? Answers to this question are just about everywhere as we think, for example, of the various types of scandals tied to both the summer and winter Olympic Games. For example, the Vancouver Province (2000) reported that the former "drug czar" of the U.S. Olympic Team, Dr. Wade Exum, has charged that half ot the team used performance-enhancing drugs to prepare for the 1996 Games. After making this statement, the response was rapid: he was forced to resign! He is currently suing the United States Olympic Committee for racial discrimination and harassment.

Viewed in a different perspective, as reported by David Wallis (2002), Dr. Vince Zuaro, a longtime rules interpreter for Olympic wrestling, said recently: "Sports are so political. If you think what happened with Enron is political, [try] Olympic officiating. ... Every time there's judging involved, there's going to be a payoff." Further, writing about the credibility of the International Olympic Committee, Feschuk (2002) stated in an article titled "Night of the Olympic Dead": "The IOC has for so long been inflicting upon itself such severe ethical trauma that its survival can only be explained by the fact that it has passed over into the undead. Its lifeless members shuffle across the globe in a zombie-like stupor, one hand extended to receive gratuities, the other held up in exaggerated outrage to deny any accusations of corruption."

***Dick Pound's Reward for Distinguished Service.*** Closing out reference to the Olympic Games Movement, recall the case of Dick Pound, the Canadian lawyer from Montreal, who had faithfully and loyally striven most successfully to bolster the Games' finances in recent decades. He had also taken on the assignment of monitoring the situation with drugs and doping, as well as the bribery scandal associated with the Games held in Salt Lake City. In the race to succeed retiring President Samaranch, Pound unbelievably finished in third place immediately behind a man caught in a bribery scandal just a short time earlier. Just punish "the messenger"...

Finally, in the realm of international sport, Dr. Hans B. Skaset (2002), a Norwegian professor, is set to make a prediction at a conference on drugs in sport scheduled for November, 2002. He will predict as keynote speaker that "Top international sport will cut itself free from its historical values and norms. After working with a clear moral basis for many years, sport by 2008-2010 will continue to be accepted as a leading genre within popular culture—but not, as it was formerly, a model for health, fairness, and honorable conduct..."

Switching venues, you don't see the hockey promoters doing anything to really curb the neandertal antics of professional hockey players. Or considering professional sport generally, note the view of sport sociologist, Steven Ortiz, who has found in his study that "there clearly seems to be a 'fast-food sex' mentality among professional athletes" (Cryderman, 2001)

In addition, in the realm of higher education, Canadian universities are gradually moving toward the athletic-scholarship approach that certain universities in the East and Midwest sections of Canada have been following for years illegally (Naylor, 2002)! In September, 2001, a Halifax, Nova Scotia team (the St. Mary Huskies) beat Mount Allison's, New Brunswick's football team by a score of 105-0. In this article, one of a series sponsored by The Globe and Mail (Toronto), various aspects of this disturbing development were considered. Interestingly, this is just "penny-ante" compared to the financial practices of various upper-division university conferences in the United States.

**How to Reclaim Sport (Weiner).** In writing about how society's obsession with sport has "ruined the game," Jay Weiner (2000) of the Minneapolis Star- Tribune asks the question: "How far back must we go to remember that sports matter?" Recalling the time when "sports had meaning," and "sports were accessible," he recommends that society can only "reclaim sports from the corporate entertainment behemoth" if it does the following:

1. Deprofessionalize college and high school sports,
2. Allow some form of public ownership of professional sports teams,
3. Make sports affordable again, and
4. Be conscious of the message sport is sending.

To summarize, the sport industry has quite simply conducted itself in keeping with the prevailing political environment and the ethos of the general public. It has not understood and consequently not accepted the contention that there is an urgent need for sport to serve as a beneficent social institution with an underlying theory looking to humankind's betterment (an "IF 'this,' THEN 'that' will result" type of approach). Thus, it could be argued that society does indeed believe that competitive sport is doing what it is intended to do—i.e., provide both non-moral and moral values to those involved. The non-moral values could be listed as recognition, money, and a certain type of power, whereas the moral values could be of a nature designed to help the team achieve victory—dedication, loyalty, self-sacrifice. If this assessment is accurate, the following question must be asked: What then does the prevailing ethos in sport competition do to help boys and girls, and men and women, to learn honesty fair play, justice, responsibility, and beneficence (i.e., doing good)?

There are continuing strong indications that the sport industry is "charging ahead" driven by the prevailing capitalistic, "global village" image of the future. Increasingly in competitive sport, capitalistic theory is embraced ever more strongly, an approach in which winning is overemphasized with resulting higher profits through increased gate receipts. This same sport industry is aided and abetted by a society in which the majority does not recognize sufficiently the need for sport to serve as a social institution that truly results in individual and social good. Thus, on the one hand there are scholars who argue that democratic states, undergirded by the various human rights legislated (e.g., equal opportunity), need a supportive "liberal consensus" to maintain a social system that is fair to all. Yet, conservative, essentialist elements functioning in the same social system do not see this need for a more humanistic, pragmatic consensus about the steadily mounting evidence showing a need for ALL people to be active physically throughout their lives.

It is argued here, therefore, that commercialized sport will have great difficulty "crossing the post-modern divide." Zeigler (*Quest*, 1996) points out that almost every approach to "the good life" stresses a need for an individual's relationship to developmental physical activity such as sport and fitness. Should not we in NASSM be assessing this social institution of sport to determine to what extent the way we present sport to our students is resulting in their becoming imbued with a desire to promote the concept of "sport for all" tp foster overall human betterment?

***Functioning With an Indeterminate, Muddled Theory***. Once again, before considering future societal scenarios that our culture is facing, I repeat my argument that today sport is functioning vigorously with an indeterminate, muddled theory that implies that sport competition builds both "moral" and "social" character traits consonant with democracy and capitalism. I am arguing further that crossing the post-modern divide means basically that we in NASSM as sport and physical activity management educators should see through the false front and chicanery of the developing economic and technological facade of the global hegemony. Face it: Sport is simply being used as a powerful institution in this "Brave New World" of the 21st century.

***Future Societal Scenarios (Anderson)*** Walter Truett Anderson (1997), president of the American Division of the World Academy of Art and Science, has sketched four different scenarios as postulations for the future of earthlings in this ongoing adventure of civilization. In this essay "Futures of the Self," taken from The future of the self: Inventing the postmodern person (Tarcher/Putnam, 1997), Anderson argues convincingly that current trends are adding up to a turn-of-the-century identity crisis for humankind. The creation of the present "modern self," he explains, began with Plato, Aristotle, and with the rights of humans in Roman legal codes.

The developing conception of self bogged down in the Middle Ages, but fortunately was resurrected in the Renaissance Period described by many historians as the second half of The Middle Ages. Since then the human "self " has been advancing like a "house a fire" as the Western world has gone through an almost unbelievable transformation. Without making this an historical treatise, I will say only that scientists like Galileo and Copernicus influenced philosophers such as Descartes and Locke to foresee a world in which the self was invested with human rights.

"One World, Many Universes." Anderson's "One World, Many Universes" version is the most likely to occur. This is a scenario characterized by high economic growth, steadily increasing technological progress, and globalization combined with high psychological development. Such psychological maturity, he predicts, will be possible for a certain segment of the world's population because "active life spans will be gradually lengthened through various advances in health maintenance and medicine" (pp. 251-253)

Nevertheless, a problem has developed with this dream of individual achievement of inalienable rights and privileges, one that looms large at the beginning of this new century. The modern self, envisioned by Descartes, a rational, integrated self that Anderson likens to Captain Kirk at the command post of (the original)!) Starship Enterprise, appears to be having an identity crisis. The image of this bold leader (he or she!) taking us fearlessly into the great unknown has begun to fade as alternate scenarios for the future of life on Eart  are envisioned. In a world where globalization and economic "progress" seemingly must be rejected because of catastrophic environmental concerns or "demands," the bold-future image could well "be replaced by a post-modern self; decentered, multidimensional, and changeable" (p. 50).

Captain Kirk, or "George W," as he "boldly goes where no man has gone before"—this time to rid the world of  terrorists)—is facing a second crucial change. As they seek to shape the world of the 21st century, based on Anderson's analysis, there is another force—the systemic-change force mentioned above—that is shaping the future. This all-powerful force may well exceed the Earth's ability to cope. As gratifying as such factors as "globalization along with economic growth" and "psychological development" may seem to the folks in a coming "One-World, Many Universes" scenario, there is a flip side to this prognosis. This image, Anderson identifies, as "The Dysfunctional Family" scenario. All of these benefits of so-called progress are highly expensive and available now only to relatively few of the six billion plus people on earth. Anderson foresees this as "a world of modern people happily doing their thing; of modern people still obsessed with progress, economic gain, and organizational bigness; and of post-modern people being trampled and getting angry" [italics added] (p. 51). And, I might add further, as people get angrier, present-day terrorism in North America could seem like child's play.

## What Kind of A World Do You Want for Your Descendants?

What I am asking here, my colleagues, is whether members of THE one North American professional society for sport management are cognizant of, and approve of, the situation as it has developed. Are we simply "going along with the crowd" while taking the path of least resistance? Can we do anything to improve the situation by implementing an approach with our students that could help to make the situation more wholesome?. More precisely, the question is, whether the North American Society for Sport Management can, and indeed should, re-orient itself to play a significant role in helping sport and physical activity become a social institution exerting a positive influence in the "adventure" of civilization.

To do this, as professionals we should determine what sort of a world our descendants should be living in. If you consider yourself an environmentalist, for example, the future looks bleak to you at present. If you are business oriented, however, continued economic and technologic growth could well be the answer to all upcoming problems. Finally, if you see yourself as something of a "New Ager," you can only hope for some sort of mass spiritual transformation to take place.

Finally, as I see it, the members of the North American Society for Sport Management are at the moment, individual and collectively, typically conforming blindly to the power structure as it uses our medium of education and recreation—i.e., sport—for its selfish purposes. As one aging person who encountered corruption and sleaze in the intercollegiate athletic structure of several major universities in the United States, I retreated to a Canadian university where the term "scholar-athlete" still implied roughly what it says. However, I now see serious problems developing in Canadian inter-university sport as well.

Two Approaches to Consider. What can this diatribe possibly mean to the members of the North American Society for Sport Management? As I see it, we have several choices before us. One choice is to do nothing. By that I mean that we continue in the same vein as we are doing presently. This would require no great effort, of course. We can simply go along with the prevailing ethos of a society that is using sport to help in the promotion of social, as opposed to moral, character traits. In the process, "business as usual" will be supported one way or the other—by hook or by crook.

A second approach, one that I recommend strongly, is that we live up to the dictates of our constitution. Permit me to remind you what Article II (Purpose) of the Society's constitution calls for. After stating that we should "promote, stimulate, and encourage study, research, scholarly writing, and professional development in the area of sport management *broadly interpreted* " [the italics are not mine]. It continues by explaining that "this statement of purpose means that the members of this Society are concerned about the theoretical and applied aspects of management theory and practice specifically related to sport, exercise, dance, and play as these enterprises are pursued by all sectors of the population "

Still further, our constitution states that "in the furtherance of these aims and objectives, the Society shall endeavor to carry out the following functions: (a) support and cooperate with local, regional, national, and international organizations having similar purposes. (b) organize and administer meetings to promote the purpose stated above, and (c) issue appropriate proceedings and journals." I don't believe it is necessary to press this point any further. At present the farthest thing from our "collective mind" would be to show steady, deliberative concern about the theoretical and applied aspects of management theory and practice as related to the other aspects of our charge in our constitution (i.e., exercise, dance, and play).

What we are showing deliberate concern about to a great extent—and doing it quite nicely—is about the theoretical and applied aspects of commercialized sport management (i.e., management quite narrowly interpreted ). This in itself is good, we might say. However, this is simply not enough for a professional society such as ours. And, to repeat, this is especially true if ones reads our constitution. What we are doing, I suggest, is devoting ourselves to the type of sport that in the final analysis means least to our society and ignoring that which could mean the most. We should be seeking the answers to such questions as (1) what is sport's prevailing drift, (2) what are the advantages and disadvantages of sport involvement for life, and (3) what is sport's residual impact on society?

Even though I was personally involved in sport competitively throughout high school and college, and then coached university football, wrestlng, and/or swimming over a period of 15 years, I have personally been conducting an informal boycott of the NFL, NBA, and NFL, and of all commercialized university sport for years. Frankly, it disgusts me, because it is basically non-educational and subversive to the higher purposes of democracy. I confess that I still watch golf and tennis on tv, but the rest of it is for the birds.

Further, I'm convinced that the commercialized Olympic Movement with its drugs, officiating, free-loading officials and bribery problems—not to mention its millionaire basketball and hockey players—will eventually suffer the same fate as the ancient Games did in 576 B.C.E. unless radical change takes place soon. The late Baron de Coubertin and Avery Brundage must indeed be "whirling in their graves" at a rate to soon exceed the sound barrier!

## Concluding Statement

You may think that I am being unduly pessimistic, that I have reached the "old-curmudgeon" stage. This may be partially true, but I urge you, the members of NASSM, to adhere—in both your research and in your professional actions— to your stated and approved purpose much more carefully than you are doing at present. I urge you further to seek the answer to two fundamental questions, The response to the first question might well cause action to be taken in the near future to answer question #2. These questions are: (1) in what ways can we accurately assess the present status of sport to learn if it is—or is not—fulfilling its role as a presumably beneficent social institution? and (2)—depending on the answer to #1, of course—will you then have the motivation and professional zeal to do your utmost to help sport achieve what could well be its rightful place in society? I believe sport and related physical activity—broadly interpreted—can indeed be a worthwhile social institution contributing to the wellbeing and health of people of all ages and conditions? As they say, "don't be part of the problem, be part of the solution!"

# References

Anderson, W.T. (1997). *The future of the self: Inventing the postmodern person.* NY: Tarcher/Putnam.

Berman, M. (2001) *The twilight of American culture,* NY: W.W. Norton.

Blinde, E.m. & McCallister, S.G. (1999). Women, disability, and sport and physical fitness activity: The intersection of gender and disability dynamics. *Research Quarterly for Sport and Exercise,* 70, 3, 303-312.

Booth, F.W., & Chakravarthy, M.V. (2002). Cost and consequnces of sedentary living: New battleground for an old enemy. Research Carmel, IN: *Benchmark. Digest* (PCPFS), 3, 16, 1-8.

Cryderman, K. (2001). Sport's culture of adultery. *The Vancouver Sun* (Canada), August 21, C5.

Depauw, K.P. (1997). The (in)visibility of disability: Cultural contexts and "sporting bodies," *Quest,* 49, 416-430

Encarta World English Dictionary, The. (1999). NY: St. Martin's Press.

Feschuk, S. (2002). Night of the Olympic dead. National Post (Canada), Feb. 16, B10.

Hahm, C.H., Beller, J.M., & Stoll, S.K. (1989). The Hahm-Beller Values Choice Inventory. Moscow, Idaho: Center for Ethics, The University of Idaho.

Huntington, S.P. (1998). The Clash of Civilizations (and the Remaking of World Order. NY: Touchstone.

Huxley, J. (1957). New wine for new bottles. NY: Harper & Row

Kavussanu, M. & Roberts, G.C. (2001). Moral functioning in sport: An achievement goal perspective. Journal of Sport and Exercise Psychology, 23, 37-54

Long, W. (2001. Athletes losing faith in hard work. *The Vancouver Sun* (Canada), Jan. 31. E5.

Lumpkin, A., Stoll, S.K., & Beller, J.M. (1999). Sport ethics: Applications for fair play (2nd ed.). St. Louis: McGraw-Hill.

Malina, R.M. (2001). Tracking of physical activity across the lifespan. *Research Digest* (PCPFS), 3-14, 1-8.

Muller, Herbert J. (1952) The uses of the past. NY: Mentor.

Naipaul, V.S. (Oct 30, 1990). "Our Universal Civilization." The 1990

Winston Lecture, The Manhattan Institute, *New York Review of Books*, p. 20.

National Association for Sport and Physical Education. (2001). The coaches code of conduct. Strategies, Nov.-Dec., 11.

Naylor, D. (2002), In pursuit of level playing fields. *The Globe and Mail* (Canada), March 9, S1.

Priest, R.F., Krause, J.V., & Beach, J. (1999). Four-year changes in college athletes' ethical value choices in sports situations. *Research Quarterly for Exercise and Sport*, 70, 1, 170-178.

Province, The (Vancouver, Canada) (2000). Drug allegations rock sports world. July 3, A2.

Rudd, A., Stoll, S.K., & Beller, J.M. (1999). Measuring moral and social character among a group of Division 1A college athletes,

non- athletes, and ROTC military students. *Research Quarterly for Exercise and Sport*, 70 (Suppl. 1), 127.

Schlesinger, A.M. (1998). (Rev. & Enl.).The disuniting of America. NY: W.W. Norton.

Skaset, H.B., Email correspondence. May 14, 2002.

Tibbetts, J. (2002). Spend more on popular sports, Canadians say, *National Post* (Canada), A8, April 15.

Toynbee, A. J. (1947). A study of history. NY: Oxford University Press.

Wallis, D. (2002). Annals of Olympics filled with dubious decisions. *National Post* (Canada), Feb. 16, B2.

Weiner, J. (Jan.-Feb. 2000). Why our obsession has ruined the game; and how we can save it. *Utne Reader,* 97, 48-50.

Zeigler, E.F. (1989). An introduction to sport and physical education philosophy. Carmel, IN: Benchmark.

CPSIA information can be obtained at www.ICGtesting.com
Printed in the USA
LVOW02s1735031213

363589LV00001B/1/P

9 781604 147438